Before

Before you see your first client

55 things counselors, therapists and human service workers need to know

Howard Rosenthal, Ed.D.

Brunner-Routledge
Taylor & Francis Group

NEW YORK AND HOVE

Published in 2005 by
Brunner-Routledge
270 Madison Avenue
New York, NY 10016
www.brunner-routledge.com

Published in Great Britain by
Brunner-Routledge
27 Church Road
Hove
East Sussex BN3 2FA U.K.

www.brunner-routledge.co.uk

Brunner-Routledge is an imprint of the Taylor & Francis Group.
Printed in the United States of America on acid-free paper.

10 9 8 7 6 5 4 3 2 1

Library of Congress Cataloging-in-Publication Data

Rosenthal, Howard, 1952–
    Before you see your first client : 55 things counselors, therapists,
and human service workers need to know / Howard Rosenthal.
        p. ; cm.
    Originally published: Holmes Beach, FL : Learning Publications,
Inc., c1998.
    ISBN 0-415-95064-3 (pbk. alk paper)
    1. Mental health counseling–Practice. 2. Counseling–Practice.
3. Psychotherapy–Practice. 4. Mental health counseling–Vocational
guidance. 5. Counseling–Vocational guidance. 6. Psychotherapy–
Vocational guidance. I. Title.
    [DNLM: 1. Counseling. 2. Psychotherapy. WM 55 R815b 1998a]
    RC466.R67 2004
    362.2′04256–dc22   2004051837

    Cover design: Elise Weinger
    Cover image: ©Lawrence Manning/CORBIS
    Author photo: ©Marilyn Wolfe

Contents

Introduction xi

1. Join Forces with a Psychiatrist to Open a
   Risk-Free Private Practice 1

2. Don't Become Married to a Single Referral
   Source 5

3. Accept the Fact That Salaries in This Field Are
   Often Unfair 7

4. It Pays to Be Assertive When You're Shopping
   for Your Salary 9

5. Managed Care Panels Often Slam the Door in
   Your Face 11

6. Managed Care Firms Dictate Who, When,
   and How 13

7. The Multicultural Diversity Secret: You Can Work
   with a Wider Range of People than You Think 17

8. Never Give Any Client Information without
   a Signed Release-of-Information Form 19

9. You Must Use a DSM or ICD Diagnosis
   to Secure Third-Party Payments 21

10. The Insurance Superbill Must Have Your Name
    as the Provider 23

11. Lecturing May Not Flood Your Waiting Room
    with Clients 25

12. Referrals Received Do Not Determine How Many
    New Clients You Actually See 27

13. Managed Care Companies Discriminate against
    Some Counseling and Psychotherapy Theories 29

14. Refer Severely Disturbed Clients for a Medical or
    Psychiatric Evaluation 31

15. Find Out Whether the Psychological and Psycho-
    Educational Test Reports You Receive Are
    Individualized 33

16. Don't Be Misled by Clients Who Initially Put
    You on a Pedestal 37

17. Most Professional Certifications Won't Help You
    Secure Insurance Payments 39

18. Don't Use Paradoxical Interventions with Suicidal
    and Homicidal Clients 41

19. Conduct a Suicide Assessment on Each Initial
    Client 43

20. Don't Try to Clone Your Favorite Therapist 45

21. When In Doubt, Use a Person-Centered
    Response 47

22. Read Ethical Guidelines Before You Even So
    Much as Hug a Client 49

23. Don't Rush to Therapeutic Judgment Until You
    Get All the Facts 53

24. The Number One Therapeutic Blunder:
    Confronting Sooner than Later 55

25. You Are Not a Failure if You Don't Land Your
    Dream Job 57

26. Your Supervisor's Knowledge and Experience
    Should Not Be Underestimated 59

27. Use Verbiage Your Client Will Understand 63

28. Be a Better Helper by Networking with Others
    in the Field 65

29. Grandfathering: The Fast Track for Snaring
    Licenses and Certifications 67

30. Use Free Advertising to Build Your Agency
    or Practice 71

31. Helpers Are Mandated Child-Abuse Reporters 75

32. Beyond Confidentiality: Professional Counselors
    and Therapists Have a Duty to Warn 77

33. If You Want to Work in a Public School, Contact
    the Department of Education 79

34. Don't Let a Day from Hell in Court Lower Your
    Professional Self-Esteem 81

35. Save Your Course Catalogs to Invest in Your
    Future 85

36. Enhance Sessions by Adjusting Group Treatment Exercises and Using Small Talk 87

37. If a Client Was Disappointed with the Previous Helper Find Out Why 93

38. Use Caution When Considering the "In" Diagnosis 97

39. Don't Go into This Field to Recount Old War Stories About Your Own Recovery 101

40. Don't Become Married to a Single System of Psychotherapy 105

41. Be Enthusiastic if You Want to Be a Better Workshop Presenter 107

42. Don't Try to Clone Your Favorite Mental Health Lecturer 109

43. If a Client You Have Been Seeing for an Extended Period of Time Requests Marriage, Family or Couples Therapy, Consider a Referral to Another Therapist 111

44. Be Prepared to Change Therapeutic Strategies at a Moment's Notice 113

45. Documentation: The Royal Road to Promotion 115

46. Avoid Dual Relationships Like the Plague 117

47. Insider Tips for a Good Cover Letter and Human Service Resumé 121

48. If You Are Daydreaming, Your Client Will Perceive You as an Uninterested Helper 125

49. Pick a Theory of Intervention and a Job You Believe In 127

50. Despite the Pitfalls, Make Friends with the Media to Promote Yourself and Your Agency 131

51. Writing a Book or Starting a Project? Ask Your Agency First 137

52. Your Employment and Credentials Determine What You Pay for Malpractice Insurance 139

53. Private Practice Is Not a Panacea for Everything That Ails You 143

54. Steer Clear of False Memory Syndrome 149

55. Create an Emotional Trophy Closet to Help You Through a Bad Day 151

Conclusion 153

Introduction

This is the book I've always wanted to write and the book I'm convinced that you — as a student or practitioner — always wanted to read. This text begins where others leave off. It provides a candid behind-the-scenes look at the field of counseling and human services that you can immediately begin using to help yourself, your agency, and your clients. You will note that since nearly everything included in these pages was learned via my experience you won't find the pages cluttered with references to journal articles or scholarly tomes.

In the mid-1970s when I entered the mental/social service arena, I was armed to the teeth with information from my college and graduate classes. I was familiar with an array of theories, the theorists behind them, and enough clinical and research concepts to fill three-and-a-half dresser drawers with my class notes.

Unfortunately, I knew precious little about the real world of helping. I guess you could say I was anything but street smart when it came to life on the therapeutic playing field. Nearly every other neophyte worker I came in contact with was just as naive as I was. I can't tell you how many times in the last few years I have lamented, "If I knew then what I know now."

This book is intended to share what I've learned about a host of important topics that are conspicuously missing from many other texts, courses, and workshops in the field. This book will not teach you about the tenets of behavior therapy, Piaget's developmental stages, or the rudiments of efficacious research. It will, nevertheless, provide you with vital practical information regarding clinical work and policy issues.

I have tried to keep this work brutally frank and I don't pull any punches. I share insider information about the good — why you could make a sizeable chunk of change by being assertive when it comes to your salary, the bad — why many psychiatrists will rarely refer to nonmedical therapists, the ugly — you can be the most qualified candidate for an agency job and still have absolutely no chance of securing it, and the politics — why managed care firms will not allow you to use some of the theories you learned in school. Please remember that if you don't like everything that I say … well, I don't like everything I say either. I'm just reporting what occurs. I don't make the rules. While I sometimes don't like what goes on in the helping professions, I feel that as a professional, or a future professional, you have a right to know. Also keep in mind that some helpers and agencies would never engage in some of the distasteful practices I share in the confines of these pages.

Like any other field, there are some really terrific people and some questionable individuals who go into the helping professions. If, for example, you have a less than desirable experience with a hospital social worker, don't automatically assume that all hospital social workers and all hospital personnel are difficult to work with. Agencies, hospitals, schools, organizations, and institutions are made up of people. Don't jump to the conclusion that a given agency or institution is bad or for that matter good based on your interaction with a single individual.

One paradoxical factor is that the good, the bad, the ugly, and the politics of helping are relative. You'll learn, for example, that the same psychiatrist who would never make a referral to you (no matter how qualified you are), will necessarily be making a slew of referrals to another nonmedical therapist who will think the psychiatrist's policy is wonderful. And why not?

As this book goes to print, the issue of managed care is undoubtedly the hottest, most controversial topic in the field. Did you know that the same managed care firms who will not allow you to use certain theories you learned in school are some of the largest employers of counselors, addiction specialists, social workers, psychologists, and other human service personnel? Hence, every coin has two sides and your perception of whether my ideas are positive or negative will undoubtedly depend on your personal vantage point. Some experts are producing books and workshops that tell you how to partner yourself with managed care while others are promoting ideas you can use to create a sane agency or private practice that is managed-care free! A practitioner, for example, who has seen clients and helpers blatantly abuse the system might legitimately cherish the constraints implemented by managed care firms. A practitioner or agency that has lost extensive business as a result of this model will most likely oppose managed care.

Recently, I gave a presentation to a group of counseling students who had received academic honors and were ready to graduate with master's degrees. The information I shared with them was a condensed version of what appears in this text. I was astonished at the sheer number of students who approached me after the lecture and told me that they had never heard *any* of the material before. Most surprising, however, was the fact that the professor who invited me to speak — who was primarily an academician, rather than a clinician — sheepishly admitted that all my gems of wisdom were also new to him. It was at this point that I knew I had to write this book. It was a necessity rather than a luxury.

You'll note that the material is replete with a generous supply of actual examples. This text will thus provide a real life education for counselors, social workers, psychologists, human service workers, and anyone else who works in a public, private, government, hospital, agency, or school, mental health, or social service setting. If you read, understand, and apply the 55 key ideas I share you will be a better helper and enjoy your work more.

The descriptions and names of clients, practitioners, and agencies have been altered to protect their identities and confidentiality. Any similarities between real persons and/or entities and the individuals and/or businesses mentioned in this book are purely coincidental.

Again, please keep in mind that most practitioners/agencies never engage in any of the various distasteful practices which I describe.

Of course, the anecdotes — both positive and negative — present only my personal experiences and imaginings and thus may differ radically from your own. The reader is urged to arrive at his or her own conclusions.

1

Join Forces with a Psychiatrist to Open a Risk-Free Private Practice

Close your eyes — yes, right this moment — and imagine this dream-come-true scenario. You decide to go into private practice. You are sitting in a nice office, perhaps some would even describe it as plush, with a large oak desk, comfortable chairs, and thick deep-pile carpeting. You have a client-friendly waiting room, stocked with the latest issues of the most popular magazines. Soft soothing background music is piped in to further relax and comfort your clients. But wait, it gets even better. You have a kind efficient receptionist who answers your phone calls, books your appointments, files your clients' charts, keeps your office stocked with pens, stationery, business cards, and even does most of your insurance paperwork. Even more impressive is the fact that you have a steady stream of referrals provided for you day after day, week after week, year after year. And best of all, everything I've described is paid for by somebody else! And in many cases that somebody else is the local psychiatrist. In other words, you're not risking a single solitary dime of your own money.

Too good to be true you say? Think again! Many counselors and therapists wrongly assume that psychiatrists don't believe in counseling, therapy, or testing and don't make referrals. The truth is, however, that many psychiatrists will do everything depicted in the aforementioned fantasy — and more — if they find a nonmedical helper they trust.

Neophyte counselors fresh out of graduate school or those who are new to private practice are often surprised to discover that some (though certainly not all) psychiatrists will only refer to a counselor or therapist with whom they have a financial arrangement. By a financial arrangement, I mean that the psychiatrist will collect a sizable amount of money for every client the therapist sees. This, of course, means that the psychiatrist could be sunning and funning in the Bahamas while you are pumping up his or her bank account by seeing clients. It is commonplace for a psychiatrist to take 40 or even 50 percent of the money collected. That is to say, if you see a client for $80, then you will receive $40 less taxes as does the psychiatrist. Since the act of "fee splitting" is often deemed unethical, the psychiatrist's attorney or accountant will generally have you sign a contract that stipulates that you are paying 50 percent for the use of the office, billing services, and the office staff. This is often referred to as a percentage cut or a percentage split.

Keep in mind that the counselor would not be getting any of these referrals if he or she was not associated with the psychiatrist in question. Moreover, it is the psychiatrist, not you, who is taking the risk and virtually paying for everything necessary to run the practice. The only thing you can lose is your time. Thus, depending upon how you look at it, these so-called percentage cuts can be a good deal for the counselor as well as the psychiatrist. Moreover, nonmedical therapists are now following in the footsteps of psychiatrists and are offering percentage cuts to colleagues — even psychiatrists — who need office space, administrative services, and/or help securing clients. The trick to securing a risk-free private practice is to be assertive. Don't be afraid to approach a psychiatrist or other professional to make your dream a reality.

2

Don't Become Married to a Single Referral Source

Ah, the good old days. Susan Gladstone can remember a time when she was proud of her private practice and rightly so. In a three-month period she once snared 148 new referrals, commendable by any standard.

The good news was that all the referrals came from a single source: the inpatient stress unit down the street. The bad news is that about two years ago the unit shut down.

Today Susan now has a caseload she can count on one hand. Three clients to be exact. Susan, like many therapists, was dependent on a single referral source for her client base. Private practitioners, agencies, and hospitals must never be dependent — or married, if you will — to one source for their clients.

Diversify. Branch out. Network, even when you're doing well, because a marriage to a single referral source is never a marriage made in heaven.

3

Accept the Fact That Salaries in This Field Are Often Unfair

Needless to say I was fit to be tied when I marched — no, make that stormed — into my supervisor two's office. I had discovered much to my chagrin that three of my workers were making more than I was as their supervisor!

My supervisor listened intently to my tale of woe and then barked back at me. "How in the heck could I feel empathy for you? I'm a supervisor two and all of my supervisor ones, including you, are making more than I am."

I had to admit I could see her point. Albert Ellis, the father of Rational-Emotional Behavioral Therapy, has warned us of the dire consequences of demanding that the world be fair and perhaps nowhere is unfairness more evident than in social service positions.

I'll never forget the day I received a call from a practicum student of mine some years ago. She had secured a master's degree with a perfect 4.0 straight-A grade point average and had secured a position as a counselor in a chemical dependency unit of a hospital.

After four years of dedicated service she came across a horrendous fact that was so shocking she almost choked. As a master's level therapist her pay scale range was from $18,256 to $24,777. The scale for counselors who were recovering from an addiction was $25,333 to $41,566. In case you missed the point, the top salary for my ex-student, and others who possessed a master's degree, was less than the lowest possible salary for an individual who was in recovery! Ouch! Worse yet, those who were recovering were not required to have any minimal level of education. Some had never graduated high school!

"I should have lied about my credentials when I took the job," she told me. "I should have told them that I dropped out of grammar school and spent the sixties whacked out on a drug high."

Although it has been years since I marched into my supervisor's office, one thing remains the same. Salaries in mental health, social service, and education are often still grossly unfair.

4

It Pays to Be Assertive
When You're Shopping for
Your Salary

Herbert Spencer was the perfect employee and everyone was sad to see him leave. After 19 years of dedicated service Herb was knocking down $33,500 a year. He was repeatedly reminded he was worth a lot more, but the agency could not afford to pay him more on a limited not-for-profit budget. It certainly sounded reasonable to Herb and he accepted the explanation regarding his salary cap like a true gentleman.

One day after Herb retired the agency began the hiring process. Ann Jefferson interviewed for the job. To say that the hiring committee was impressed would be putting it mildly. There was only one problem. Although the salary range of the job was listed at $25,000 to $33,500 (Herb's salary), Ann made it clear that she had no intention of taking the job for under $35,000.

The verdict? Ann began the job making $1,500 a year more than Herb who spent a major part of his career serving the agency.

Is this fair? No, but as you know, salaries are often unfair in this field. Do the Herbs of this world know this goes on? Rarely, and if they did they would generally feel used and cheated.

Although large agencies, hospitals, clinics, and government jobs may have salary ranges that are set in stone a lot of sites in this field decidedly do not. Therefore, it is imperative to remember that it always pays to be assertive when shopping for a salary. Also, never forget that you (and perhaps even Ann Jefferson) could truly be superior to the former employee such as Herb, despite his or her years and years of service.

The bottom line on this one is crystal clear: If you're worth more money, say so!

5

Managed Care Panels Often Slam the Door in Your Face

Marty was armed with prestigious credentials — a Ph.D. from a private school, a state counselor's license, and a certification in mental health.

During the day Marty works for the men's counseling center at a large hospital. Here he is qualified to see clients from the Brand X Health Care plan. At night, he has his own little private practice. Since the Brand X program is extremely popular, Marty gets a sizable number of calls from clients at his own practice who belong to the program. When Marty called Brand X to verify insurance benefits he was told that he was not a bona fide provider when performing therapy at his private practice office.

Simple enough, he thought. I'll merely apply as a provider from my private practice address. Much to Marty's chagrin, he was rejected as a provider! Marty screamed foul play. How could he possibly be qualified at one location but not another when the contract clearly stated that it was not based on ancillary services?

Marty's story is not atypical. Several years ago I was a consultant for a large hospital. Needless to say, the hospital employees I consulted with had considerably less experience and credentials than I. Nonetheless, some of the same insurance companies and managed care programs that paid the hospital handsomely for outpatient services rejected me as a private practice provider. The moral of the story is that large agencies and influential hospitals often land up on provider panels that will reject you or your agency as a provider.

One managed care organization had rejected me on numerous occasions with the excuse that there were "too many providers in my zip code." I was repeatedly told that if someone dropped out they would let me know so I could fill the slot. One day the therapist in the office next door to me, who told me she had "connections to get in," as she put it, dropped out of the program. I immediately (say 30 seconds later) picked up the phone and called to get placed on their panel. When they gave me the song and dance routine about "too many therapists in my zip code," I told the gentleman I overheard my colleague calling him to drop out just seconds prior to my call. After stumbling over his words, the fellow suggested that perhaps they had miscalculated the numbers of helpers in the zip code and he promised to get back to me. Well I'm glad I didn't hold my breath because that was about two years ago and I still have never received a phone call.

Managed care — like salaries — is often about as fair as playing poker with a card shark who plays with a stacked deck.

6

Managed Care Firms Dictate Who, When, and How

As a provider on a new panel, Linda Lewis was pleased when she immediately received a referral. Her new client, Debra, was 14 years old and highly disturbed. Since Linda's contract stipulated that she could only see the client two times she called the managed care company.

"There's nothing to worry about, Ms. Lewis," the woman on the other end of the line assured her. "If you read the fine print in your contract you'll discover that you can request six additional sessions for Debra if you need them."

"But what if perchance I can't cure her in eight sessions?" Linda protested. "Debra really has some severe problems."

After a brief moment of silence, the woman responded. "Look I shouldn't tell you this but we track everybody on a computer. And well ... if you take over eight sessions you'll never receive another referral from us."

Linda proceeded to treat the young lady in an appropriate fashion using more than eight sessions and she has never received another referral from the company.

Here are some things managed care can dictate and the concomitant responses you might hear from them in regard to these issues:

- Who can you see. "The client must see somebody on our panel."
- How many visits are acceptable. "Your client is eligible for six more sessions."
- When the visits must occur and how much you can charge. "The six visits must take place between July 9 and October 11 and you can only see the client once per week. M.S.W.'s receive $65 for a 50-minute session." Never mind the fact that your customary charge for this service is $80. The managed care firm — not you — will set the fee!
- What service is appropriate. "You can use psychotherapy, but not biofeedback."

Many providers in this field consider managed care the enemy, yet it does have a positive side. First and foremost, managed care companies hire a large number of counselors and therapists. In addition, prior to the era of managed care, clients often stayed in treatment for lengthy periods of time that were unwarranted to say the least. Other clients received treatment modalities not considered ideal, since the counselor was not accountable for his or her actions. Most of the practitioners I have spoken with admit such blatant abuse of the system ran insurance costs up and was not the best thing for the patient. These same practitioners usually agree, nevertheless, that managed care's current policies such as extremely short hospital stays, and its over-emphasis on brevity in terms of outpatient treatment, has gone too far in the opposite direction.

Perhaps what we need is a system that espouses a balanced middle-of-the-road philosophy.

7

The Multicultural Diversity Secret: You Can Work with a Wider Range of People than You Think

My past experience as a supervisor of child abuse and neglect workers taught me an important lesson about diversity. I would routinely get calls from African-American clients who wanted white workers. When I asked why, the answer I usually received was the African-American workers were usually "too hard on their own people." Interestingly enough, I would also routinely receive calls from Caucasian clients who would vehemently insist that they wanted an African-American worker. When asked, they explained it was because "African-American workers do more for their clients."

Were these glittering generalities about Caucasian and African-American workers really true? Sometimes perhaps, though certainly *not* in every case. The point nevertheless is that you shouldn't assume that Native Americans, Asian Americans, or anyone else automatically wants a helper with a similar racial or ethnic background. Clients sometimes intentionally request someone who is different. Although this won't be true in every case it behooves us to learn more about diversity and cajoles us to face clients from other cultures with an optimistic attitude. You can work with a wider range of people than you think.

8

Never Give Any Client Information without a Signed Release-of-Information Form

I often tell my students that release-of-information forms are a helper's best friend. You should always have a supply of them on hand. If you do field work, carry a supply in your car, purse, or brief case.

When someone asks you for information concerning a client, or anytime you wish to receive feedback regarding a client from a source other than the client, you will need a release-of-information form signed by the client.

In fact, you will often need several of them for a single client. Say your client saw a therapist before seeing you. You might wish to secure that therapist's records or talk with that particular therapist by phone. A release is required.

Perhaps the same client's attorney calls you and your client wants you to talk with her. Again, a release is necessary. Perhaps your client is taking medications prescribed by a psychiatrist and you want to confer with him to coordinate the treatment. You will need the client's signature and a separate release form for each of the three situations.

Never photocopy the signature and check the dates on such forms. Release-of-information forms will generally only be applicable for a given period of time.

Another hint is that when somebody requests information from you (by sending you a signed release-of-information form, of course), you should only release information and data collected by you and/or your agency. For example, as a counselor perhaps you acquired medical information on your client from his chiropractor. You could not release this to a party requesting information on your client. If the party requesting the information insisted that he needed the chiropractic assessment (which might well be legitimate), then your client would have to sign a release for the party in question to send it directly to the chiropractor. If you or your agency didn't collect the information first hand, you are not permitted to give it to anyone else.

9

You Must Use a DSM or ICD Diagnosis to Secure Third-Party Payments

When I asked 16-year-old Matthew Briggs why he cursed out his math teacher and tossed a rock into the school trophy closet, he said, "Oh, heck. That's easy. I'm ADHD (Attention Deficit Hyperactivity Disorder) and my psychiatrist told me I've got a chemical imbalance that causes depression." Matthew had the psycho-babble lingo down pat.

Many counselors and therapists often worry about the effects of labeling a client and they darn well should. Some clients — like Matthew — use the label as an excuse for acting in a dysfunctional manner. In some cases the diagnosis or label simply becomes a self-fulfilling prophecy. The worst scenario is the so-called iatrogenic illness, a term borrowed from medicine to describe a physician-induced illness. Thus, when a helper erroneously tells a client that he or she has a given illness and the client believes he or she suffers from it, then an iatrogenic illness has been instilled.

However, if you are looking to get paid for your services, third-party payers such as insurance companies, managed care firms, Medicare and Medicaid require a diagnosis from the Diagnostic and Statistical Manual (DSM) of the American Psychiatric Association or the International Classification of Disease (ICD) produced by the World Health Organization.

Many therapists who are aware of the danger of differential diagnosis try to straddle the therapeutic fence by giving the client an innocuous diagnosis such as "Adjustment Disorder." Unfortunately, some third-party payers will not accept diagnoses such as this that are not serious. In other cases, third-party payers will not allow the helper to refer the client for hospitalization in an emergency without a "more disturbed" condition. Translation: Change the diagnosis and they'll give you what you want!

In a computerized global economy, where a diagnosis could indeed follow a client around like a dark cloud, a helper who despises differential diagnosis will find himself or herself in a dilemma.

10

The Insurance Superbill
Must Have Your Name as
the Provider

A recent newspaper article reported the story of a social worker who spent the night in jail. She didn't pull off a bank job nor did she hold up an armored car. Instead she put somebody else's name as the provider on the insurance bill she gave to the client because the insurance carrier in her state would not reimburse a social worker's services.

The person who actually performs the therapeutic service must put his or her name on the insurance bill given to the client and/or the third party such as an insurance company. You may not get paid as often, but I can assure you, you'll sleep a lot better!

11

Lecturing May Not Flood Your Waiting Room with Clients

Try this creative visualization exercise. You've just given the best lecture of your professional career to a audience of several hundred people, many who could benefit from your treatment services. You are convinced your business is ready to boom. You even contemplate moving to a larger office in order to accommodate all the new clients you'll be serving.

Giving presentations is wonderful publicity for your agency and/or your practice. You will be informing as well as helping others. Lecturing helps to curb pernicious burnout and increases the size of your practice.

Do not, however, rush out to purchase an SRO (Standing Room Only) sign for your office. Here's why:

Typically after administering an effective presentation — especially to a large audience — you will have a sizable number of individuals who will want to use your services

25

or make referrals. The most common scenario, nevertheless, is that the referrals from your public appearance will sporadically trickle in. You could receive two referrals on the day after the lecture, none during the next four weeks, then perhaps three in the next month. You may even receive an occasional referral years after your talk. I know I have.

The referral pattern following a lecture generally resembles water dripping from a leaky faucet rather than a dam that has burst. There will even be times when the phone never rings after your self-proclaimed award-winning performance.

If you do give a presentation and find your appointment book exploding at the seams, then consider yourself fortunate, but your experience is the exception rather than the rule.

12

Referrals Received Do Not Determine How Many New Clients You Actually See

Jerry was the top referral source for the local crisis center. In a single month 51 clients were referred to Jerry's conveniently located private practice. However, by the end of the month Jerry only received two inquiries regarding his counseling service. One of the individuals made an appointment and never returned for a second session.

Jerry was baffled. With over 50 bona fide referrals in less than 30 days he expected his practice to grow quickly. In order to put his dilemma in perspective he called his long-time friend Pat who had been the center's top referral source some years ago. Pat chuckled and informed Jerry that his track record had been even more dismal. Out of 54 referrals he received during his final month as a provider, only one client telephoned to inquire about services and she never made an appointment.

To be sure, some referral sources have clients, such as those mandated by law, who follow through better than others.

The old business philosophy that suggests a transaction isn't complete until the check clears the bank or you have the money in your hand is also true in mental health. A good rule of thumb is that you shouldn't count your referrals until you have a warm body in front of you asking for assistance.

13

Managed Care Companies Discriminate against Some Counseling and Psychotherapy Theories

In graduate school, I was taught to pick an intervention theory I had faith in and felt comfortable using. It seemed like good advice — until I began working with managed care and had to make a living.

You see, when you fill out an application to become a managed care provider one of the questions you will be asked is what treatment modality you use. I can promise you that 99.9 percent of the time if you put something like person-centered, nondirective, Rogerian, psychodynamic, existential, or psychoanalytic your chances of being accepted as a provider are almost nil.

Managed care programs are typically based on the principle of cost containment. Translated this means brief, strategic, and short-term therapy. When you keep the therapy short the managed care firm shells out less money. Therapies that encourage you to build an extensive relationship with the client such as person-centered counseling, or those that espouse delving into one's past and/or digging up repressed memories, do not lend themselves to a maximum of six or eight treatment sessions. Such paradigms often assume that the client will be coming for months or perhaps even years.

Many applications directly ask what percentage of clients you usually successfully treat in a given number of sessions. For example, what percentage of clients do you terminate in six sessions or less? Ten sessions or less?

Unfortunately when a client is rushed through treatment he or she often returns again and again for assistance. In reality, much to the chagrin of the managed care firms, it might actually take less sessions and cost less money to take the time necessary to treat the client once and treat him properly.

Nevertheless, the rule for getting on managed care panels at this point in time is really quite simple. Keep your application brief!

14

Refer Severely Disturbed Clients for a Medical or Psychiatric Evaluation

I don't need to possess a crystal ball or be a mind reader to guess what most nonmedical practitioners are thinking about this suggestion. "No way. I'm not referring my client to a psychiatrist or a medical doctor. They are just pill pushers. They'll just fill my client up with Prozac, Zoloft, Paxil, or the drug of the month. That's what they do with every client. They don't know anything about counseling."

Perhaps medical mental-health providers are prescription pushers. Nevertheless, imagine how you would feel if your client did indeed have a physical problem. Your client could be the victim of blood sugar fluctuations, low thyroid, or an organic neurological difficulty. If you don't fancy the idea of a law suit and want to rule out an organic problem that could abate depression, find a medical practitioner you trust and make the referral.

15

Find Out Whether the Psychological and Psycho-Educational Test Reports You Receive Are Individualized

Laura Swanson had a strange look on her face as we perused the test summary pertaining to her youngest son Mike. She looked so perplexed I finally inquired about her nonverbal messages.

"It's just so eerie," remarked Mrs. Swanson. "I guess it must be genetics." Mrs. Swanson was referring to the fact that two years before when I sent her oldest son Joey for testing the results seemed almost identical.

Since I had seen literally hundreds of clients I couldn't remember the exact results of Joey's psychological workup. I waited until the end of our session to pull his file. Much to my chagrin Joey's psychological report wasn't similar to

Mike's, it was identical except for the first paragraph. After my initial shock, I contacted the psychologist who did the testing to find out exactly how this could have happened.

The psychologist explained that the battery of tests was indeed administered to each client and the scores tabulated but, with the advent of computer word-processing programs, reports were no longer truly individualized.

Since writing the test reports is a lengthy and arduous process only the first paragraph, that is to say, the one that talks about the client's age, appearance, reason for referral, and effort put into the administered tests, is 100 percent tailored to the actual client in question. The rest of the paragraphs are selected from a number of choices written prior to the testing and designed to "kind of, sort of, fit any client," as the psychologist put it. For the second, third, fourth paragraphs, and so on, the psychologist will pick between 12 to 15 paragraph choices based on test results. Thus it would not be unusual after a while to have several clients with one or more identical paragraphs; or in the case of Mike and Joey, two completely identical psychological reports.

When I protested that the procedure was dehumanizing and not individualized, the psychologist noted that with the computerized method a psychometrician could work a lot less, complete numerous reports in a short period of time, help more clients and make a greater sum of money.

I began referring my testing to another individual only to discover that she was using the same computerized write-ups. I've also spoken with a couple of school psychological examiners in elementary and secondary schools who also use this questionable procedure.

Not everyone who administers tests uses this paradigm to complete the reports. Nevertheless, if you don't have the time or the expertise to do your own testing and don't feel comfortable with the pick-a-paragraph system of psych work-ups, I suggest you talk to the person who does your testing about this issue or find another individual who does not engage in this practice.*

---

* Let me emphasize that my commentary in this section refers to a written test battery, i.e., summarizing of a number of tests. Many popular tests now offer computerized scoring and/or test summaries of a client's performance on a single measure and this practice is ethical in every respect.

16

Don't Be Misled by Clients Who Initially Put You on a Pedestal

"Look, I've just got to tell you this, Dr. Norton. You're a genius. No, I really mean that. Look, I've been to seven other therapists — and rather good ones I must add. Dr. Gleason, of course, studied with Rogers when he was alive, and Dr. Kent spent a great deal of time out in California with Perls. But the amazing thing is that I've made more progress in two sessions with you than I made with all of them put together. I can't believe nobody else ever used a behavioristic approach. What can I say? You're wonderful. I feel like I wasted the last 12 years of my life going from one inept therapist to the next. I don't know what I would have done if I hadn't met you."

There is a small chance that this client truly feels that Dr. Norton is a therapeutic genius as well as his psychotherapeutic savior. There is also a greater chance, however, that this client is playing what I like to call the Pedestal Game. Here is how the game works.

The game begins with a client who has a sack full of problems and is looking for a knight in shining therapeutic armor. During the initial interview this type of client will systematically lambaste all his or her previous therapists. You'll hear tip-off comments such as:

- "All my ex-therapist ever did was talk about her own problems."
- "My previous therapist never really gave me any advice. I'm not sure what he did to help me."
- "I went for years and never accomplished anything."

Then the client — as in the case of Dr. Norton — will shower you with praise and of course place you on a pedestal well above any of the incompetent helpers in the past. The sad part of the game, however, is that in a short period of time you can — and probably will — join the ranks of the incompetent crowd. In fact, in a short period of time your client could be seeing another therapist and lavishing him or her with praise using the same lines you heard during the initial session.

Hence, a word to the wise. Don't pat yourself on the back until you're certain you won't fall from your pedestal.

17

Most Professional Certifications Won't Help You Secure Insurance Payments

You've seen the ads in the professional newspapers and newsletter promising increased professionalism and added certification letters following your name. It seems with each new issue in the professional publications another certification is being offered. Ideally, you would probably like to be a member of all of them but time, money, and credentials will no doubt dictate the ones you chose to secure.

When I speak with neophyte counselors I often hear that the primary reason they are trying to snare a certificate is to enhance their ability to secure third-party and insurance payments. My advice is to save your time, money, and ink to fill out the generally lengthy application. In 20 years of private practice I have never received a single dime of income based on an acquired certification. Insurance companies are interested in state licenses — counseling, psychology, or social work — period.

I have heard that this could change in the coming years, initially in the area of substance abuse counseling.

Snaring a certification may increase your knowledge, professionalism, status in the eyes of your clients, and networking abilities, but it won't do one iota for your bank account. As for the future? I personally hope this chapter becomes obsolete in the near future.

18

Don't Use Paradoxical Interventions with Suicidal and Homicidal Clients

You've probably seen it many times at the movies and on television. There's a distraught man standing on the twenty-seventh story of the highest building in the city. He's familiar since you've seen individuals like him grace the silver screen in the past. He's depressed — so depressed he can't imagine going on with his life. Below, a crowd of bystanders gathers, their eyes glued on him. The police chief bellows through his megaphone as he tries to dissuade this poor soul from ending his life. The place is swarming with the SWAT team and hostage negotiation squad.

Then the action begins. The hero (usually an irate rule-breaking police officer or private detective) swaggers out on the ledge. Our suicidal fellow whose life is on the line is shocked. Who is this guy and what's he doing out on the ledge with him? Is he crazy or what? Next instead of talking this poor soul out of it he offers to push him, jump with him, or hand him a weapon so he can put himself out of his misery. The suicidal individual is so taken aback he decides not to jump after all. The crowd is ecstatic, except for the police chief who warns the hero never to do that again.

Now that we've covered the tinsel-town version, let's analyze what would occur in a real-life situation if you urged a suicidal person to "go ahead and do it" perhaps in the confines of an individual counseling session. Chances are the depressed fellow would jump, shoot himself, or kill both of you! Moreover, if he survived the attempt or successfully killed himself and the family found out how you handled the case, the chances are good — no make that excellent — that you would be in store for the malpractice suit of your life.

Does paradox work? You bet it does and it often works extremely well as a therapeutic ploy. A client who is too nervous to give a speech in front of his college class is told in therapy that he should *purposely* shake as much as he can and try to make a fool of himself. The result will often be that he is calm and steady. Paradox is an excellent technique. Nevertheless when a life is on the line and you're dealing with a suicidal, homicidal, or suicidal/homicidal client the person's will to live and judgment are waning. In such cases the rule of thumb is simple: Avoid paradoxical interventions and reverse psychology like the plague.

19

Conduct a Suicide Assessment on Each Initial Client

Don was taken aback when his supervisor questioned him about asking his client if she was suicidal. "Of course not," replied Don, "I don't want to put the idea in her head. Besides, she came to learn behavior modification strategies to help her give up smoking."

Don has decidedly taken the wrong action. A good rule of thumb is to ask every client if he or she is suicidal regardless of their presenting complaint. To this day, I am still surprised by the sheer number of clients who forthrightly say "yes" to this question. A high percentage of such clients come to the therapy room with innocuous complaints such as weight loss, smoking, or lack of assertiveness.

Generally, suicide is the eighth leading killer of all Americans and the second or third leading killer of teens and college students. It is estimated that one in 10 individuals will make a suicide attempt before age 19. The geriatric suicide rate is more than double what it is for the nation as a whole.

A simple, yet effective five-step plan for dealing with suicidal behavior is:

- Ask every client if he or she is suicidal. It won't put the idea in their head.
- If the client has a plan, try to circumvent it. You could, for example, have a family member remove pills or a firearm. (Just for the record, 65 percent of all suicides — more than all the other methods put together — involve guns or rifles.)
- Contract with the person to stay alive. (If the individual will not sign a behavioral contract or agree to a verbal contract then refer the client to a hospital setting.)
- Rule out organic factors by referring the client to a psychiatrist or other medical doctor.
- Make certain that the client continues to receive psychotherapy.

20

Don't Try to Clone Your Favorite Therapist

I will never forget the excitement I felt after I read the book *Uncommon Therapy* which depicted the therapeutic genius of Milton H. Erickson. I wanted to be Erickson for my clients. After all, they deserved the best and most efficacious treatment — a Milton H. Erickson clone if you will.

I picked a client in my caseload who seemed similar to one Erickson had treated in his book: an eighth-grade male who seemed to be responding quite well to a Rogerian approach. Nevertheless, I anticipated that his treatment program would be even more efficacious after I began implementing an Ericksonian intervention. I memorized Erickson's verbiage for my client's next session. Just to make certain I didn't miss a beat I placed a copy of Erickson's interventions behind my desk so I could refer to it if necessary.

One of the youngster's teachers had heard positive things about my work and accompanied my client to the session. The teacher felt she had information that could be clinically significant and she wanted to use my services for other youngsters with emotional difficulties.

Since Erickson was extremely forceful with his client (actually, belligerent might be putting it more accurately), I decided to do the same. Unfortunately, as I started to read my Ericksonian script my client did not respond in a positive manner. Instead, he ran out of my office crying and he never returned. His teacher said she was appalled by my therapeutic tactlessness and informed me that she would never refer anybody to me.

Lest the reader assume that I was cured of my Milton H. Erickson clone fascination, I must admit I was not. I was convinced that my client's reaction had been a fluke, and that nearly any other client would have responded in a positive manner. Several months later I used a verbatim transcript of one of Erickson's hypnotic dialogues with a client I was seeing for stress reduction. The client noticed that I was using a new technique and stated toward the end of the session that although the new procedure was somewhat helpful, he wholeheartedly favored my traditional approach as better.

Looking back on my Ericksonian clone experiments I now see my mistakes. First, no two clients are the same. Although I thought my clients were similar to Erickson's they were certainly not identical. And secondly, my personality and personal attributes are different than his. In fact I am convinced that if Erickson had actually been seeing my clients he would *never* have chosen the techniques or hypnotic inductions that I inappropriately implemented. The essence of his genius was precisely that he worked with each client as an individual.

21

When In Doubt, Use a Person-Centered Response

If you're a golfer you've no doubt heard the old saying that asserts, "When in doubt, use a five iron." That is not bad advice. For those of you who don't hit the little old white ball around let me explain this gem of wisdom. A five iron does not hit the ball a long distance like some other clubs. Neither does it have the accuracy of other clubs to hit the ball a short distance. Basically, a five iron is a middle-of-the-road club — in between everything else. It has a fair degree of accuracy and allows you to hit the ball a fair amount of distance. Because of this, golfers who are unsure what club to use are often told to rely on the trusty five iron. No, it won't give you spectacular distance like a long iron or a wood or a pinpoint bull's-eye accuracy like a short iron, but on the other hand it won't do anything too extreme to damage your score.

Therapy is a lot like golf. There are many times when even the best therapist is sitting there with no idea — I mean absolutely none — how to respond to the person or persons in the session. Sure you could rely on silence and a few "uh-hums," but a strict reliance on such responses can be frustrating for many clients.

Over the years (after making literally hundreds, maybe thousands, of therapeutic blunders) I learned that Person-Centered Rogerian Therapy is a lot like pulling out your trusty old five iron. In other words, it's a safe bet. A person-centered response generally won't produce bells, whistles, magical cures, or insights that take your breath away. But, like a five iron, it won't cause any damage either. You won't, for example, usually see a client bolting out of the office as was the case in my aforementioned Ericksonian clone experiment.

One day I was talking to a highly trained clinical psychologist who had a practice next door to mine about this principle and told him that I was a bit perplexed that this advice never seemed to be forthcoming at seminars and workshops in the field. My colleague merely shrugged his shoulders and replied, "That's easy. Good therapy is slow, rarely dramatic, and often boring. Nobody wants to pay to see that at a workshop." And so it goes.

The next time you're in a therapeutic bind forget about confrontation, a wild clinical hunch, or a bogus Freudian interpretation. Your therapeutic person-centered five iron — composed primarily of paraphrasing and reflection — will go the distance toward helping your client.

22

Read Ethical Guidelines Before You Even So Much as Hug a Client

The late 1960s and early '70s was an era characterized by the "summer-of-love," bell-bottom pants, long hair, and the philosophy espousing you to "do your own things as long as it doesn't hurt anyone else." Then there was psychotherapy — encounter groups, rolfing, physically stroking clients, and hand massages. Any therapist worth his or her salt gave each and every client a fatherly or motherly hug. And why not? The human touch was and still is comforting. Some research even indicates that it is physiologically beneficial.

I'll never forget a graduate internship I served with a professor in his private practice. It was my first day and my professor ran up to a female and gave her a hug so powerful he nearly lifted her off the ground. As the woman walked into the therapy room I asked my professor in a whisper whether the woman was his wife or his sister. He looked at me like I had experienced a psychotic break from reality and said, "Howard, that's our four o'clock client. This will be our first co-therapy session together."

I have an interesting audio tape recorded in the 1970s from a local college library that I often play for my students. On the tape an experienced male therapist states that he does not believe in sexual contact with female clients. The female therapists on the tape actually argue with him and express their viewpoint that displaying sexual behavior toward female clients could be beneficial.

But times change and it seems the pendulum has swung to the opposite end of the therapeutic spectrum. I routinely ask my students and those I supervise or consult whether hugging a client is ethical. The answer I usually get is something like, "Get serious. Of course, it's ethical and it's therapeutic for my clients. It's not like I'm having sex with them or anything."

In the state where I live and work, hugging is considered an ethical violation just like having sex with a client. When I first came across this fact in the ethical guidelines, I called my licensing bureau to see if clients had filed misconduct charges against counselors for hugging. The director of licensing said that clients had contacted the licensing bureau to complain about such behavior.

When I explain that such behavior is deemed unethical the response is often, "Show me. I don't believe it!"

This "show me" attitude is precisely my point. Practitioners should read the ethical guidelines set forth by their state licensing board or professional organization.

Moreover, if you take a close look at your malpractice insurance I can almost assure you it has a stipulation that if somebody files a sexual claim against you it will either be paid at a lesser rate than normal or your insurance carrier will not back you at all.

So although bell-bottom pants and sixties platform shoes are making a comeback, the same cannot be said for touchy, feelie, huggy therapeutic interventions.

23

Don't Rush to Therapeutic Judgment Until You Get All the Facts

It was Brett Park's first day as my supervisee and it was quite evident he was trying to impress me with his therapeutic judgment and his clinical savvy. As Amy, a 32-year-old teary-eyed female in our hospital group talked about her tendency to feel trapped, Brett glanced at me and lifted his eyelids as if to say, "I know exactly what's troubling her, watch me put her out of her misery." With his holier-than-thou mentality, he abruptly interrupted her.

"Amy, Amy. Stop. What I want to know is why are you staying in a relationship with a man who physically abuses you? Why don't you get out?"

Amy as well as the other members of the therapy group looked spell-bound. "What?"

Again Brett checked eyes with me to make certain I was witnessing his city-on-a-hill interpretation of the century.

"Amy I repeat, why are you staying in a relationship with a man who is abusive?"

I knew what was coming but I figured Brett needed to learn a lesson and he'd find out soon enough anyway.

"Brett," she said sheepishly, "I'm not in a relationship with a man, I'm a lesbian."

Think back to when you were a teenager and you were trying to act really cool and impress somebody. Most likely you did appear really cool until you did something stupid like spilling a soda on your date or walking face first into a closed door.

Brett later admitted that he felt foolish for not waiting to secure all the facts, not to mention the fact that he obviously hadn't read the client's hospital chart. The worse part was that Amy told me privately that she immediately lost faith in him as a therapist because he seemed to be analyzing her situation before he knew anything about her.

Don't try to be a guru or a palm reader because I can almost assure you that sooner or later you'll end up with a face full of tea leaves! Listen to the client and by all means resist the temptation to rush to judgment. You'll be a much better helper and you'll avoid a slew of bumps on your forehead.

24

The Number One Therapeutic Blunder: Confronting Sooner than Later

I have to chuckle when I hear new students talking about what makes a counselor an effective helper. The following statement is a generic version of something I frequently hear.

"Man, I'll tell you that therapist is a lot better than all the rest. I mean he got right up in that guy's face and chopped him down to size with a few well-chosen curse words. It was fabulous. The therapist was yelling so loudly you could hear him in the next suite of offices."

Not only is this style of combat intervention not good therapy — it probably isn't therapy at all. Helping isn't about "chopping the client down to size." Most of us know at least one spouse, son, daughter, boss, teacher, or mother-in-law who can do that quite effectively.

A landmark movie loosely dubbed the *Gloria Film* (the actual name is *Three Approaches to Psychotherapy*) is illustrative of this fact. Gloria, the client, is given a brief psychotherapy session with the three greatest living therapists at that time: Carl R. Rogers, Albert Ellis, and Fritz Perls. Rogers was kind and empathic to Gloria. Ellis came across somewhat didactic and intellectual. Perls on the other hand was sarcastic, overly confrontive, and quite belligerent. During the first few minutes of the interview he forthrightly called Gloria a phony for smiling when she purported that she was nervous. When she was interviewed after the movie, Gloria asserted that overall she liked Perls the best. Years later, however, she reflected on the experience and stated that Perl's intervention was psychologically damaging and had a profound negative impact on her.

Please don't misunderstand me. It is certainly appropriate to confront your clients. However, I would suggest to you that in terms of confrontation, timing is everything. A confrontation that would be inappropriate during your initial meeting with the client could be right on target during perhaps the eighth or tenth therapy session. When I took back I am convinced that the number one factor that produced disastrous outcomes resulted from confronting clients too quickly and with too little tact.

In most cases the rule on confrontation is simple. Later is nearly always better than sooner.

25

You Are Not a Failure if You Don't Land Your Dream Job

Molly went to the job interview and felt like she just hit the ultimate grand slam of her career. The interviewer seemed thoroughly impressed with her answers. Molly thought her interview went perfectly — perhaps even a little too perfectly.

Two days later Molly was horrified when she received a rejection letter in the mail. Molly did what nearly every other job applicant would do in a similar situation. She began soul searching in an attempt to discover what she did wrong or what qualities she lacked. Perhaps she needed another course in group work? Maybe her answers were shallow regarding interventions with resistant clients. Perhaps she should have worn her gray pants suit instead of her dark blue one to the interview. In essence, she was certain that she did something wrong. She whipped out her mental baseball bat and emotionally beat herself to a pulp.

What the Mollies of this world usually don't stop to think about is that agencies often promote from within, and that she never had a chance at the job. Nevertheless, to keep things ethical and honest, many agencies, hospitals, and practices run ads for the job in the newspaper, send copies of the job description to college and university job bulletin boards, and apprise the state employment security office of the opening.

How will you know if the job will be filled from within? You won't. But you should still do your best in the interview because (a) there might truly be a job opening, (b) the person they have slated for the job could leave unexpectedly and they will need an outsider to fill the position, and (c) they may decide they really like you and have another position for you.

Do the best you can on each and every job interview. Just remember that if things go a little too smoothly, the interviewer may secretly have somebody else groomed for the position. Thus don't blame yourself and feel free to wear the same color pants suit or slacks to your next interview.

26

Your Supervisor's Knowledge and Experience Should Not Be Underestimated

As a caseworker, I routinely interviewed my clients in their homes, but Mr. Burton requested a session at our office. Over the phone he sounded as if he was at the end of his rope and I acquiesced to his request for an office visit. He was crying crocodile tears as he told me about the abuse his wife was inflicting upon him. I was highly empathic and my heart went out to this man as he recounted tales of physical abuse. Quite frankly, I was beyond the point of empathy. I felt sympathy for my client.

My diagnosis was simple. He was a battered husband and in a period of psychotherapy when behavior therapy was king, I decided that the only sensible treatment of choice for this man was assertiveness training. I couldn't wait for my morning meeting to share my thoughts with my supervisor.

I was certain she would approve my plan of action so I could turn this man into an assertive individual who could finally stand up to his wife.

During my supervisory session I recounted the specifics of my meeting with Mr. Burton. My supervisor listened intently and it was obvious that she was hanging onto every word. Finally she spoke.

"Howard," she said, "listen to me. This man is dangerous, very dangerous. And I have no doubt that he could hurt or perhaps even kill his wife and children. You need to advise Mrs. Burton to get out now. Do you understand me?"

Did I understand her? Quite honestly I thought she was nuts. I had just explained how this man was the victim and my supervisor had the audacity to suggest he could be a perpetrator and a batterer. I was bewildered. Where in the world was my supervisor coming from? Perhaps she needed a little psychological help herself!

My best friend, who was also a brand new caseworker at the time, wholeheartedly agreed that Mr. Burton needed assertiveness training. Over a hamburger, fries, and a shake at lunch we both came to the conclusion that my supervisor was incompetent despite her vast experience. Her directives provided us with a great belly laugh.

When I returned from lunch I had a message to call the FBI. It seems that Mr. Burton had beat up his wife, took the kids over the state line, and was holding them at gun point with his old M-16 army rifle! The FBI was calling me for a personality profile. What in the world was I going to say? "Oh, gee, I just think the guy needs to learn a little assertiveness training so he can stand up for himself."

I guess I don't even have to mention that I felt even more inept when I visited Mrs. Burton at her home and discovered that her husband broke three of her ribs before he took off with the kids.

I learned two important lessons that day. One, I needed to take my supervisor's vast knowledge and experience seriously. And, two, maybe when she talked, I needed to listen and take her advice.

27

Use Verbiage Your Client Will Understand

I was one of six professionals participating in a foster-care permanency planning and review team. We were staffing the case of 12-year-old Doris Hollander. Both she and her father, Bob Hollander, were present.

As we discussed whether Doris should return home, we tossed around numerous psychological and social work terms. During this hour-and-a-half session the abbreviated term "division" was used for the Division of Family Services repeatedly.

Suddenly Mr. Hollander, who had been laconic, stood up and began yelling. "The division this, the division that. I'm sick of this. We've been here for over an hour and that's all you've talked about. If we're not gonna talk about poor little Doris, and have to discuss arithmetic, can't we discuss subtraction, multiplication, or addition? We've been talking about nothing but division."

A thorough check of the record indicated that Mr. Hollander was virtually illiterate, uneducated, and mentally retarded. He truly had no idea what we were talking about.

Thus, in Mr. Hollander's mind, division was a mathematical term, rather than an abbreviation.

It reminds me of the old story about the hypnotist. He's hypnotizing a patient and thinks he's doing rather well. Just as the hypnotist is convinced that the patient is in a trance state, the patient opens his eyes and blurts out: "Hey, Doc, by the way, what the heck does cataleptic mean?"

When working with clients make sure that you explain all the lingo, technical jargon, and/or abbreviations that you are using. Two CB radios must be on the same channel to effectively communicate. Why would you assume that the helper/helpee relationship is any different?

28

Be a Better Helper by Networking with Others in the Field

Sue Spector's clients have a distinct advantage over the other clients in her geographical service area. Sue's clients, who have no place to stay, are allowed to spend six days in the local shelter for the homeless. Other helpers' clients are only allowed three days. Her clients routinely seem to get better food orders, clothing allowances, and see their workers at the local mental health clinic faster than clients served by others workers.

Sue Spector isn't smarter or more educated than her peers. And she's not courting an influential politician or businessman. She has, nevertheless, mastered the fine art of networking.

Networking has also been beneficial for Wayne Sills. On three separate occasions Wayne has been able to land a job in a day or two when hospital mergers eliminated his position over night. His colleagues are still lamenting and spending the better part of the day searching for job leads.

Roughly speaking, networking is the act of making work-related contacts with others in the field. You can network by attending conferences, workshops, fund raisers, or social service award banquets. You can network by getting to know your professors and practicum instructors better. In fact, the people who are the most adept at networking are those who are sophisticated and creative enough to use the technique in almost every situation.

It would be impossible to overestimate the power of networking for your clients, yourself, your practice, or your agency. So often it's not what you know but who you know through networking. Have you done your networking for today? If the answer is "no," then pick up the phone and make contact.

29

Grandfathering: The Fast Track for Snaring Licenses and Certifications

In the state where I practice, it might surprise you to learn that thousands of social workers don't even have a bachelor's degree in social work. Some have never even taken a course in the field. I know scores of others with Ph.D.'s who have been told they cannot even sit for the psychology licensing exam, while I know one licensed clinical psychologist who has a bachelor's degree and some graduate work.

The whole thing sounds crazy. How could people with little or no credentials secure licenses and/or certifications while others who are armed to the teeth with knowledge and experience have the door slammed in their faces?

The answer can be neatly summed up in one term: grandfathering. The term "grandfather clause" refers historically to a procedure enacted by some Southern states in which a literacy requirement for voters was waived for those whose forebearers voted before the Civil War. Today, in the fields of mental health and social service, a grandfather clause forbids you from practicing a given profession, such as psychology, and/or using a given title, such as certified addiction's counselor, unless you were practicing prior to the enactment of the legislation.

What this means in plain everyday English is that when a new license or certification is introduced there is usually a window period in which practitioners can sneak in with credentials that would not be acceptable at a later date.

Take the social workers mentioned earlier. Currently, in the state where I practice, a social worker would need an M.S.W. from an accredited school, postgraduate experience, and a passing score on the social work exam in order to be licensed. During the grandfathering window period, however, basically all that was needed was experience in the field.

Every year in my undergraduate Introduction to Human Services classes I teach the necessary criteria to enter the different professions. Without fail, someone comes to the next class and says something like, "Hey, my neighbor is a psychologist, counselor, substance abuse specialist, marriage and family therapist, social worker etc. etc. and she doesn't meet those requirements you're talking about."

Of course, nine out of 10 times the student is correct: Her neighbor jumped on the bandwagon immediately and was grandfathered in. Hence, the irony is that many, if not most of the professionals who were wise enough to take advantage of grandfathering, would not be eligible to practice based on their current qualifications.

So what does this have to do with you? If you see a license or certification that you believe could even remotely help your career — either now or in the future — then my advice is to take action and apply for it immediately. Don't wait. Grandfathering periods are often short and if you blink

— or think about it too long — you could miss your golden opportunity.

A word of caution is in order, however. A certificate or license obtained via grandfathering is *not* always equal to a certificate or license earned via the procedures required in the post-grandfathering stage. Take the social workers I mentioned earlier who are licensed, but do not have M.S.W. degrees. Many of them have discovered that insurance companies and managed care firms (who may indeed be greedy but are hardly stupid) are familiar with the grandfathering procedure. Thus, social workers in our state who submit insurance claims as providers are often told: "Oh, you are a Licensed Clinical Social Worker, that's great. Send us a copy of your M.S.W. degree or transcript." Of course, at that point in time, the party is all over. One social worker who grandfathered in without an M.S.W. told me that she has never been accepted on a managed care panel nor has she ever been reimbursed for performing therapy.

Grandfathering did, nonetheless, allow her to legally throw up a shingle and offer her own fee for service practice.

30

Use Free Advertising to Build Your Agency or Practice

You can be the best service provider or the finest agency in the world but if nobody knows about you it will not matter. There are two key reasons why this contention is of the utmost importance. The first is because nobody can benefit from your expertise, and secondly that your agency will soon be going out of business.

Many helpers admit they could care less about marketing. They often forget the obvious: clients and referral sources must be aware of your services in order to use them.

There was a time — and not that long ago — when professionals outside of the mental health and social service arena who marketed themselves or their agencies were the exception rather than the rule. Times have changed. Dentists, chiropractors, and attorneys routinely spend huge sums of money marketing their services. For example, a group of attorneys in a large metropolitan area told me that one single ad on the back cover of the telephone directory costs them over $65,000 (gulp) a year. And that doesn't include the rest of their phone bill.

In our field, hospitals and large corporations are taking interstate billboard ads, telephone yellow pages space that rivals attorneys, and sometimes even television and radio spots.

Unknown to many helpers — even some seasoned professionals — press releases are a way to compete on a small scale. Direct-mail marketing experts call press releases "free advertising."

In case you didn't know it, anybody can send out a press release — you don't have to be an actor, a multi-billion dollar corporation, or a U.S. Senator. Your only investment costs are for envelopes, stamps, and the paper they are printed on.

You can send a press release to literally any media: television, radio stations, and periodicals such as magazines, journals, professional newsletters, and newspapers are the most common sources.

Statistically speaking, most press releases sent out in our field come from book publishers and professional organizations, however, I must re-emphasize that you can send them out on your own to announce anything new, such as an upcoming event, new program or service, change of address or name, additional personnel, promotions, or even an employee of the month.

Perhaps you are starting a relapse day-treatment program for cocaine addicts. Maybe your agency created a hotline for those who are experiencing panic attacks. Your practice could be integrating biofeedback to help athletes combat stress. Any or all of these programs could be the subject of a press release.

Creating a press release is simple. First, target your source and call to find out the person to send your release to. If there is a special section of the paper you want your release to appear in, you could address the envelope to reflect your choice, for example, *The Daily Herald News, Mental Health Helps Column.*

To write a press release you simply begin with the words "press release," the date, and the name and number of the contact person at your agency or practice. Then type a description of who you are and what you are doing. Short press releases that are double-spaced, less than a page, and sound newsworthy are most likely to get published. For example, several years ago I sent out one that began: Noted therapist/author opens a private practice in West County. Several of the freebie neighborhood publications in my area ran the release as did the largest paid daily newspaper. I might add that I've had excellent success with professional newsletters distributed nationally when I've written a new book or created a relevant audio program.

It is important to know that media sources are not obligated to publicize your press release. Moreover, the media source will not inform you when and if the release is published, therefore it will be up to you to spot it. Lastly, a wallet-size black-and-white photo of yourself will sometimes be used via the media source if you are so inclined to send one. Regardless of whether the release runs or not, your photo will not be returned to you.

31

Helpers Are Mandated Child-Abuse Reporters

When Lou began working for the agency he boldly announced that he didn't believe in reporting cases of child abuse to the authorities. "It degrades the relationship I have built with the family," he explained.

Unfortunately, Lou wrongly assumes that he has a choice in the matter. Professional mental health and social service personnel are mandated reporters — they must report to the state child abuse hotline all suspected cases of physical abuse, neglect, sexual abuse, and exploitation. It's the law.

What's more, all reports must be filed in a timely manner. I recently read about a case concerning a counselor who discovered on a Friday that a child was being sexually abused. The counselor reported it the first thing Monday morning. Sadly enough, the child was abused over the weekend and legal action was taken against the counselor.

Turning one's head on abuse/neglect situations is detrimental to the helper's welfare, as well as the client's. A school principal once boasted, "We don't have any abuse in my school, if you know what I mean. We don't need the negative publicity in my school district." Several weeks later it was discovered that one of his pupils was being severely abused. The news media — the very people he wished to avoid — rushed in to find out why he had not been on top of the situation and reported the abuse. Thus in an attempt to avoid bad publicity, his inaction fostered it and endangered a child's life.

Remember: Report each and every suspected case of child abuse and neglect. It's the law.

32

Beyond Confidentiality: Professional Counselors and Therapists Have a Duty to Warn

There was a time when you could tell your therapist anything and it was confidential, but a 1974 landmark precedent-setting case changed all that.

A client named Prosenjit Poddar went into a college counseling center and said he was going to kill his girlfriend, Tatiana Tarasoff, when she returned from vacation. The psychologist at the center believed him and thus sought the guidance of his supervisor. The supervisor was also convinced that the gentleman was serious and contacted the campus police. The campus police said that they knew Poddar and did not consider him a serious threat. Not long after, Poddar brutally murdered Tarasoff.

Tarasoff's parents were incensed. They contended they could have protected their daughter if she had known she was in danger. The parents thus sued the university (*Tarasoff v. Regents of the University of California*) and lost. The parents — convinced they had a valid point — appealed the case. The decision was overturned by the state supreme court. The supreme court ruled that a therapist has a duty to warn an intended victim.

Because of the Tarasoff case and subsequent cases that reaffirmed this decision, nearly every ethical code for counselors, psychologists, social workers, and addictions specialists advises helpers to take reasonable action in cases where suicide or homicide are evident. Every helper is urged to break confidentiality in order to save a life. Check your state's licensing ethics or your professional organization's ethical code regarding this important issue.

33

If You Want to Work in a Public School, Contact the Department of Education

Lisa knew what she wanted to do in life and thus enrolled in the local master's degree program at a private university in order to reach her goal. Two years later she received her degree in counselor education and was in hot pursuit of her dream: A career as a school counselor in an elementary or secondary public school.

Much to her chagrin and shock she was told during her first job interview that she did not meet the qualifications for the position. Worse yet, she was informed that with her qualifications she would not be qualified for the position of counselor at *any* public elementary or secondary institution.

What Lisa was unaware of — and many others like her — is that public schools are under the auspices of the state department of education.

Here is the question I routinely ask my undergraduate students who are first entering the field. Could I secure a job as a counselor in a public school? I have a doctorate in counseling, I'm a licensed professional counselor, and I have a number of national certifications.

The answer, like Lisa, is that I too am unqualified for such a position. The reason is that in the state where I live the Department of Elementary and Secondary Education requires that school counselors must work as school teachers for two years. Although that particular requirement is hardly true in every state, it is true that state departments of education set certification standards for positions in public schools. Often these standards are totally different than the standards that are set for licensed practitioners working in public, private, agency, or hospital settings. The courses and experiences can be mutually exclusive from those set by the Board of Healing Arts, the Department of Economic Regulation, or any other body that governs licensed healers.

Looking at it from the other side, a school counselor would not necessarily be licensed as a counselor and therefore could not work in private practice. A certified school psychologist or school social worker might not be licensed to practice outside the public school and the licensed psychologist or social worker would not necessarily have the credentials to work in the public school system.

If your goal is to work in a public school, contact the department of education in your state *as early in your career as possible* and make certain — unlike poor Lisa — that you fulfill their requirements. Private schools and colleges are exempt from department of education certification requirements, however, there are indeed private schools that make such credentials mandatory for employment.

A journey of a thousand miles starts with the first step. Make certain your first stride is in the right direction!

34

Don't Let a Day from Hell in Court Lower Your Professional Self-Esteem

Bonita was one of the most competent therapists I knew. She was well-trained, had a wealth of experience, and she was a leader in the area of sexual abuse treatment. As she left the courtroom, she appeared somewhat like a soldier coming home after being beaten in battle. Tears streamed down her cheeks as she told me how incompetent she felt. In a fit of sadness, hurt, and anger she said, "I don't know if I will ever practice psychotherapy again. Perhaps that attorney was correct, maybe I don't know what I'm talking about."

Poor Bonita was responding to the intense verbal beating she had sustained just moments earlier in the courtroom. I was present and I had to admit it wasn't a pretty sight. Bonita, an M.S.W. social worker, had little training in the area of psychological testing. The attorney who opposed her client asked her numerous intricate questions about the projective Rorschach Ink Blot Test. Bonita, who had never been trained in testing, was unable to answer any of his questions. When this happened the attorney merely laughed, shrugged his shoulders, rolled his eyes, turned to the judge and sarcastically said: "And she calls herself an *expert witness*. Give me a break."

Years later, I personally experienced a similar situation. I was testifying as an expert witness for an adolescent who was seemingly suicidal while living in her father's home due to his tendency to be abusive. The father, who wanted custody and desperately wanted to keep the child in his home, hired a pit-bull attorney who decided he was going to make mince meat out of me that day — which he did.

He began by asking me whether I was aware that the young lady had been treated for a cavity several days before I had interviewed her. I truthfully admitted I was not. He then asked me whether I was familiar with an antiquated obscure study and he listed the names of the researchers. Once again, I was honest and conceded my ignorance. On doing so the attorney proclaimed that the study conclusively demonstrated that dental work exacerbates depression and, needless to say, that affected my assessment of the client. He then leaned toward me with an eyeball-to-eyeball stare intended to instill a high degree of shame and uttered, "And you call yourself an expert witness. Ha!" One thing was for certain. Either I was experiencing *déjà vu* or the attorney was wining and dining the lawyer who had gone for Bonita's jugular vein.

After seeing what happened to Bonita, and experiencing it myself, I decided to ask my own attorney how attorneys are so adept at lambasting a helper's professional self-esteem, and how helpers can inoculate themselves from this legal intimidation.

My attorney suggested that it is generally quite easy to lower a professional helper's credibility. The attorney merely looks for a weakness in the witness' training. In Bonita's case it was simple. Social workers often possess little or no training in psychological testing, especially projectives like the Rorschach. In my case, the attorney banked on the fact that as a nonmedical therapist I had never had a single course in dentistry. And ... surprise ... surprise ... he was correct. My attorney even suggested that on occasion a lawyer might actually contact a therapist who is not involved in the case to help him or her choose a little-known therapeutic fact that the witness is not cognizant of. Pretty sneaky, huh?

Anyway, my attorney suggested that the only way to inoculate one's self is to do so psychologically. That is to say, you should be eminently prepared for your day in court but must realize that the opposing attorney usually can and will intimidate you by asking questions that you and most likely none of your peers with similar training would have a chance of answering.

Make a vow to yourself that you absolutely, positively will not allow any attorney to take away your professional self-esteem. Say to yourself, I'm okay but I'm not sure about that attorney.

35

Save Your Course Catalogs
to Invest in Your Future

The state licensing board told Larry they might accept his course, Vocational Center Counseling, based on the catalog description. Since Larry had completed the course in 1971, and since the school could not find the catalog, Larry was fortunate that he had saved an original copy at home. Despite the fact that the paper was turning a funny shade of yellow, the licensing bureau decided that this old course met the requirements for licensing.

There are several reasons to keep your course catalogs. The first is that names of courses and course descriptions change over the years. In order to justify a course for state licensing, certification bodies, or teacher certification, an explanation of the course is often required. As a teacher in a college I admit that 99 percent of the time your college or university will be able to find and copy a page from the original catalog. However, I have come across several instances such as Larry's, in which the school was unable to produce the catalog or the original description. It is rare but has been known to occur.

Another reason to keep the original catalog is that program requirements change over the years. If you have an original catalog you can prove to the school administration that you met the current requirements for graduation when you began your course of study. Some — though certainly not all colleges, universities, and graduate schools — will honor the requirements that were relevant when you began the program. Thus, this principle usually applies to part-time students or those who had to drop out for a while and therefore have been in school for an extended period of time.

Course catalog descriptions are often worth keeping especially if you are transferring to another school and wish to sell the new school that your previous course, despite the fact that your course had a radically different name, is nonetheless equivalent to the one they want you to shell out time and money to take.

Some schools and licensing/certification bodies won't even accept a course catalog description on the basis that it doesn't give enough information. In order to satisfy these tight-fisted folks I recommend you consider the possibility of keeping a file filled with your course syllabi and outlines. This will allow you to share your readings, topics covered in the course, and assignments required.

36

Enhance Sessions by Adjusting Group Treatment Exercises and Using Small Talk

Years ago the professor for my group counseling courses suggested what seemed like the perfect interactive experience for my daily 11 o'clock stress unit hospital group. Group members were given a list of 10 individuals, five males and five females, with a brief description of each. The group then had to agree on five people to take to a new planet to start a new civilization. Most of the group participants at this particular hospital were factory workers and the male clients were a tad chauvinistic to say the least. It didn't take a specialist in group work to see that all the female members were literally sitting quietly outside the circle and were not participating in the group exercise. It was painfully obvious even to the untrained eye.

The male comments seemed to be reinforcing this configuration. "We need manpower for the new planet. These guys will need to lift heavy rocks and perform intense labor as they build new structures." Another male added, "Of course we'll need someone who is tough to protect us and keep everyone safe." On several occasions the males reluctantly admitted that a female would have to "come along for the ride" — meaning for the purpose of procreation.

Although the guys loved the exercise exactly as it was outlined by my professor, I was convinced that the experience had to be tweaked to encourage female participation; not to mention the sexist attitude of the men in the group.

Thus the next time I ran the exercise with a hospital group I made a few salient changes. First, I replaced one of the 10 characters with a super macho 450-pound world champion wrestler. The guys were going to love it. He would definitely make it into the top five. Definitely, that is, until they read the description for the tenth choice. My new choice for number 10 was a female CIA sharp-shooter, with top security clearance, and extensive expertise in the martial arts. Best of all, my description of choice number 10 explained that she actually beat the 450-pound wrestler in an exhibition match of hand-to-hand combat.

This time around the females were sitting where they should rightly sit — in the circle. Choice number 10 gave them power and spawned tremendous interaction in the group.

Whenever you use a group exercise — whether it is one you learned from a textbook, a professor, a supervisor, or a workshop — don't be afraid to alter it to meet the needs of your particular client population. This principle is often applicable to exercises utilized in individual treatment as well. Unlike the old computer punch cards and modern credit card bills, group experiences usually work best if you bend, fold, and mutilate them to fit the people you are working with.

Another way to enhance your sessions is to use small talk to build rapport with your clients. For example, Jamie's mother sat in my office and said, "As I think I explained over the phone, Dr. Rosenthal, Jamie doesn't want to see you. He doesn't think he has a problem. So I guess what I'm trying to say is that on the way over here in the car he said he's not going to talk to you. I hope we didn't waste our time coming here today. He really needs the help, you know. All he talks about, Dr. Rosenthal, is that stupid car he's saving up to buy. I don't know. I suppose it's hopeless."

"Wait a moment, Mrs. Wilson. What about that stupid car he wants to buy? Can you tell me anything about it?"

"Oh, gosh. I don't know. It's some stupid old Pontiac, a 1965. Let's see, I think he called it a GTO. Why?"

"Mrs. Wilson, I've got good news for you," I told her. "I think Jamie is going to talk. In fact, I think he's going to talk a lot."

I went to the waiting room and called Jamie's name. Since my office was quite a distance from the waiting room I began my opening remarks before he ever entered the therapy room.

"You mom tells me you've got your eye on an interesting '65 Goat. (Goat is slang for a Pontiac GTO. I'm banking on the fact that Jamie will know this.) Is the 389 (the size of the engine) a single four barrel (the carburetor), or is this one equipped with tri-power (three two-barrel carburetors)?"

Jamie spoke. "Um, it's a single four barrel. Those tri-power goats are rare you know."

"Yeah, well I used to have a '65 Olds 442. That's the same body as the Goat."

Now Jamie seemed to be hooked. "Hey, that's cool. A 442. What engine did yours have?"

Jamie could now see that his therapist wasn't some big bad wolf who knew nothing about him. We both had something in common — a mutual interest if you will. We both appreciated classic 1960's muscle cars. And since we had something in common he decided he could talk to me which he did.

When I first began in this field I was taught that small talk had little or no place in the therapeutic process. I have found time and time again that it not only has a place but it is often the only way to build rapport with a resistant client. Let me give you another wonderful example.

A mother brought her son to me for therapy. Like Jamie, he told his mom he planned to remain uncommunicative and wasn't going to talk to some "stupid counselor or therapist." Actually, as you become experienced in this field you will discover that this attitude is not that uncommon, especially among children and adolescents.

The youngster sarcastically told his mother that the only way he would consider speaking with me was if I could help him secure a stereo power amplifier. Little did this child know that I personally knew a great deal about stereo equipment and before my interview with him was over I gave him directions to an obscure pawn shop where he indeed did secure the type of power amplifier he was looking for.

Obviously, not every case will go as smoothly as the two I have depicted. Helpers, nevertheless, will do well to look for a way to engage the client, especially if he or she is resistant. A knowledge of the subject matter is helpful. Although you cannot possibly know everything about every conceivable subject, even a minimal amount of information will help abet efficacious intervention. Often you can guess what topics will come up. Adolescents routinely take an interest in rock music, movie stars, and sports. When I worked closely with a managed care firm that services automotive assembly employees (and their kids, such as Jamie) I tried to keep up with trends in the automotive industry.

And how can you build rapport if you are totally ignorant regarding the subject at hand? Simple. You ask questions about it. Clients frequently feel more at ease when they can express *their* expertise during an interview.

You can secure your ideas for small talk from parents and caretakers, the case history in the client's file, jobs, or merely asking the client what he or she likes to do. Try this technique when building a good solid therapeutic relationship with a client. I have this notion you'll discover that small talk really isn't so small after all.

37

If a Client Was Disappointed with the Previous Helper Find Out Why

If a client was dissatisfied with his or her past helper I want to know why and you should too. Here are some typical statements you will hear from clients who were displeased consumers of psychotherapeutic services and strategies you might try to make their experience with you a more productive one.

Complaint: My therapist talked too much and told me what to do.

Possible remedy: Try listening more, talking less, and being a bit more nondirective or person-centered in terms of your therapeutic style.

Complaint: My counselor just sat and stared at me. He never said anything and never gave me any direction.

Possible remedy: Talk more. Be more active-directive. The father of behavior therapy, Andrew Salter, had clients of this ilk in mind when he wrote that helpers who couldn't give advice would be more useful to society as elevator operators.

Complaint: All my helper ever talked about was her own problems.

Possible remedy: Stop yapping and start listening. You've taken the principle of self-disclosure too far. If it seems difficult to stop talking about the trials and tribulations of your own life consider seeing a therapist yourself! (See idea number 39 for additional insight regarding this issue.)

Complaint: All we ever did was analyze my childhood.

Possible remedy: Try using an ahistoric or so-called present-moment approach that focuses upon the here and now. Behavioristic techniques could be appropriate.

Complaint: We never really talked about the past. All we ever did was talk about the present. I need to know how I got to be this way.

Possible remedy: If you are qualified try utilizing a psychodynamic approach that focuses more on the past and one's childhood. Steer clear of behavioristic methods.

Complaint: My therapist was too philosophical. I never really understood what I was supposed to be doing or learning from our sessions.

Possible remedy: Give the client behavioristic homework assignments and focus on cognitive-behavioral skills. Reality Therapy and Rational-Emotive Behavior Therapy could well be the treatment of choice for such individuals.

If something didn't work maybe it's time for a change.

38

Use Caution When Considering the "In" Diagnosis

I humorously tell my students and supervisees that I can remember a time when nearly everybody I knew was wearing a neck brace. Perhaps you remember it too. Whiplash was as commonplace as mom's apple pie. Then there was the era of hypoglycemia. Everybody was depressed and acting a little crazy because they were gulping down too much sugar which in turn caused low blood sugar or hypoglycemia. Even the legal profession picked up on it and the so-called Twinkie Defense was born, i.e., he committed the crime because he ate too much sugar laden junk food.

Recently more and more clients seem to fit the borderline personality diagnosis. And currently in the geographic area where I practice, kids are labeled ADHD (Attention Deficit Hyperactivity Disorder) by the droves. One of my students works in a preschool where over 50 percent of the kids are diagnosed and subsequently medicated for ADHD.

Can we go too far with the "in" or avant-garde diagnoses? I say flatly that we can and I would like to share a few examples. A psychiatrist proclaimed as an ADHD specialist was asked during a lecture how she diagnoses kids so quickly in her office since she sees so many children each day. "I don't really," replied the doctor, "I assume that if the teacher sees ADHD behavior and sends the kid to me, he or she is correct. The condition is so prevalent." I'm happy to report that numerous teachers in the audience took offense to this position and didn't appreciate being put in the position of psycho-diagnostician.

I once telephoned a psychiatrist to see if he would evaluate my client for possible medication. I did not mention any diagnosis, much less ADHD. "If it's a typical kid with ADHD that needs Ritalin (a medicine often prescribed for this condition), I'll see him," replied the psychiatrist. "Otherwise I really wouldn't have time to help."

It's really easy to fall into the trap of fitting a given diagnosis — even when it isn't the "in" diagnosis. I recently read a list of behaviors to 66 students in my undergraduate class, Introduction to Human Services. Unbeknownst to them I had read the DSM criteria for ADHD. Nearly every student had all the necessary behaviors to take on the label. Perhaps even more amazing was the story told to me by a professor in a medical school. He claims that when the AIDS epidemic first broke out he read the World Health Organization's symptoms of AIDS to literally hundreds of students without telling them what illness the symptoms corresponded to. Nearly everybody he read them to came up with a positive diagnosis!

The point is certainly not to deny that whiplash, ADHD, hypoglycemia, and borderline personality disorder exist. Such conditions do exist and no doubt in fairly high numbers. If, however, nearly everybody who crosses your path ends up with the diagnosis of the month, then it's time to give up sugar, take the neck brace off, and do a little introspection.

39

Don't Go into This Field to Recount Old War Stories About Your Own Recovery

Sally is 23 and single. Since her agency does a great deal of marriage counseling, her greatest fear is that a new client will inquire whether she has personally tied the knot. George, on the other hand, works at a child guidance clinic. His worry is that clients may become alarmed should they discover that he has no children. Craig is apprehensive that the clients in the chemical dependency unit will discount his input if they are privy to the fact that he has never been a substance abuser.

I have some surprising yet pleasant news for Sally, George, and Craig, based on my 20-plus years of clinical experience. Don't lose any sleep over it. I can remember when I personally had precisely the same concerns. What I discovered, however, was that my clients were so preoccupied with their own concerns that they rarely, if ever, grilled me in regard to my personal life.

Don't get me wrong. I firmly believe that a married couple has a right to know if their counselor is married. A mother struggling with the terrible twos certainly has a right to ascertain whether her helper has done the same, and an alcoholic is within his boundaries when he inquires about your history concerning a battle with the bottle. In fact, I feel that such clients are justified in asking for another helper if you don't possess the proper "life credentials."

I learned early in my career that although a client has every right to inquire about such particulars, only a few ever do. In general, clients are a lot more interested in overcoming their own difficulties than they are about the fact that you are single and have never raised a toddler.

I'll never forget my initial experiences in terms of self-disclosure. Even when my disclosures were concise, it was not unusual for a client to change the subject back to his or her personal situation and, in some cases, the client would interrupt me to do so.

The aforementioned phenomenon explains why clients do not want to hear long-winded stories about your own recovery. Some self-disclosure is indeed therapeutic. Nevertheless, when you go on ad nauseam about your own past I can almost guarantee you that the client (or clients, if you work in a group setting) will find it boring, distasteful, and hardly conducive to effective treatment. In essence, if you are roughly the opposite of Sally, George, and Craig, entering this field primarily to talk at length about the gory details of your own recovery, you will be sadly disappointed.

If you feel compelled to go on with endless tales of woe — you know those long-winded how-I-got-high-on-LSD-in-the-sixties sagas — about your own struggle for improvement, then let me suggest that countertransference has set in. My advice would be to find a good therapist and go pour your heart out. Clients come to talk about themselves. The rule of thumb regarding self-disclosure is that while a little bit is good, a lot isn't necessarily better.

40

Don't Become Married to a Single System of Psychotherapy

An accomplished behavior therapist was treating a woman who was convinced beyond a shadow of a doubt that behavior therapy was superficial. The woman expressed a desire to "do it right." She was certain that she needed a form of psychodynamic therapy, most likely full-fledged Freudian psychoanalysis. The woman expressed her discontentment again and again, but the behavior therapist kept reassuring her that behavioristic methods were superior.

When the woman's protests became overwhelming, the therapist suggested he would give her strict Freudian analysis for six sessions. He told her that she would have to sign a behavior contract (how's that for a paradox?) indicating that if the analysis didn't work, he would go back to a behavioristic approach. The behaviorist fully expected that the "depth psychology" treatment would be a dismal failure.

The client signed the contract and the new treatment paradigm was underway.

The behavior therapist, who possessed absolutely no training in psychoanalysis,* told the client to free associate. At other times he focused on her dreams and made interpretations about her formative years and her unconscious mind. At the end of the six sessions the woman was symptom free and did not feel the need for additional treatment.

Does this saga prove that behavior therapy is inferior to classical Freudian analysis? No, but it does illustrate that one form of psychotherapeutic intervention will not work in every case. The therapeutic strategy that worked wonders for your nine o'clock client will often fall flat on its face at 10. In fact, the modality that worked so well for your nine o'clock client this week could very well be a disaster with that *same* nine o'clock client next week. If you must be married to a single system of psychotherapy or counseling, try to be as flexible as possible within the confines of that particular modality. I often tell my students that I wouldn't trust my life — or my clients' lives — to any one system of psychotherapy.

---

*This treatment was performed about 20 years ago. Ethical guidelines currently suggest that helpers should not treat clients utilizing modalities in which they have no training.

41

Be Enthusiastic if You Want to Be a Better Workshop Presenter

I had completed a two-day mental health workshop for elementary and secondary school personnel. As I was packing up my materials to leave the building a woman, who appeared to be in her early sixties, approached me.

"Dr. Rosenthal," she said, "I just wanted you to know how much I enjoyed your presentation. In fact, I must say candidly that you gave the best speech I've heard in over 25 years of this field."

Was I pleased? Of course, I was ecstatic. Who wouldn't want to hear praise like that from a highly experienced teacher who came across so sincere?

"What was it that you liked so much?" I asked. Was it my statistics? Was she impressed with my theoretical notions or rigorous therapeutic recommendations?

"Oh, heck no," she replied, "I could have learned that stuff from any text book. It was your enthusiasm that was so striking. I believe I lost mine years ago and you rekindled it in just two days."

On another occasion I gave a lecture at a local college and a professor liked it so much she offered me a teaching job. When I asked her what caught her fancy she noted that I came into the room like a tornado. "You were just so enthusiastic," she added. Just for the record, I took the teaching job.

On another occasion my zeal landed me a free trip to Las Vegas to give a keynote speech for an international organization.

Enthusiastic lectures and workshops can open professional doors for you, in terms of building your reputation and your practice (or that of your agency), and help those who reap the benefits of your wisdom. Remember that it's not what you say, but the way you say it that often makes all the difference in the world.

42

Don't Try to Clone Your Favorite Mental Health Lecturer

I hired Farrah because I couldn't keep up with the requests I was getting for my suicide prevention speeches. The game plan was simple enough. Farrah, who had a great deal of expertise in self-destructive behavior patterns, would tag along with me for say five or 10 lectures. By doing so she would not only familiarize herself with the material but could also emulate my speaking style.

After about two weeks Farrah had committed my modus operandi to memory. She knew the material, the jokes, the silences, and even the vocal inflections. Then came the big day. Farrah got in front of her first audience, a private girl's high school, as I sat watching. As Farrah began to lecture, the young ladies instantly began to squirm in their seats. A few were beginning to nod off and one young lady in the front row was sleeping so soundly her snoring was nearly as loud as Farrah's voice.

When we processed what had happened Farrah was bewildered. She indicated that she was certain she did every-thing precisely the way I would have done it. I suggested that she was correct, but that perhaps *that* was the problem. Farrah had her own personality and her own style. Since she knew the material I admonished her to be herself the next time she was called on to present. From that point on Farrah became an adroit lecturer in her own right.

Never lose sight of the fact that your personality is dif-ferent than anyone else's. Farrah came across poorly when she tried to be my clone. Remember what happened to me earlier in the book when I tried to clone Milton Erickson? My personal attributes were obviously a lot different than Erickson's.

When a therapeutic or workshop technique works for one person it may need to be bent, folded, or mutilated, just like the group exercises I mentioned earlier, to meet your own needs and the needs of your clients or audience. Just say no to therapeutic and presentation clone experiments.

43

If a Client You Have Been Seeing for an Extended Period of Time Requests Marriage, Family or Couples Therapy, Consider a Referral to Another Therapist

Lloyd Weber had been counseling Donna Clayton for a little more than four years. During that time she made numerous improvements in her life. As she put it, she would be "forever indebted" to Lloyd for his help. Initially, Donna was certain she would leave her husband Sid. She rejected the idea that the marriage was salvageable as well as the possibility that marriage counseling could be helpful. After all, the way she described the relationship, Sid was lazy, aloof, an inept parent, and emotionally abusive. As Donna began to perceive the situation differently, she and Lloyd agreed that marital counseling might be the treatment of choice after all.

In a short period of time the flavor of the sessions changed for Donna. During a phone call, she said to Lloyd following their initial session as a couple:

"I feel hurt and betrayed. I thought you were on my side, but now I can see that I thought wrong. I can't believe your comment implying that at times I'm a bit abrasive. I'm not the one who is verbally abusive. It's Sid! I'm not the one who shirks my duty as a parent. It's Sid! I can't believe it. One session and he's manipulated you. Now you think I'm the problem. I never should have trusted you. You're just like everyone else who is fooled by his charm."

The therapist had fallen out of good graces with his client. Is this situation atypical? I think not. Although I would concede that it does not occur in every instance, it happens more than most seasoned helpers would care to remember.

Agreeing to see a client's significant other, after you have seen the client for an extended period of time, is one of the most pernicious therapeutic blunders I have encountered. The client who has built a powerful long-term relationship with the counselor — like Donna — often feels that the therapist is no longer on her or his side.

My advice to helpers faced with this dilemma is really quite simple. If you have any doubt whatsoever that the treatment could go downhill when you begin seeing a significant other, then don't. Instead enlist the help of a fellow counselor whom you trust and refer such cases out. In most cases it is best to continue to see your client while the couple's counseling is ongoing. Perhaps, your fellow colleague could even reciprocate and refer his marital and couples counseling to you.

44

Be Prepared to Change Therapeutic Strategies at a Moment's Notice

Thirteen-year-old Gloria suffered from Trichotillomania, a condition in which the client pulls out his or her hair and then on occasion eats it. Gloria was described by her mother as "unusually perceptive" and "brilliant."

I began the initial interview using a strict nondirective, person-centered paradigm. I felt I was doing a superb job until she introduced the fact that the treatment wasn't going anywhere fast. In fact, it was going nowhere.

Gloria said, "You know. Every time I say something, you kind of repeat it in your own words and you seem to understand exactly what I feel. And you're very kind, sincere, and caring. But that isn't all there is to counseling, is it? I mean we both know you are going to do something different to help me stop pulling my hair."

I didn't know whether Gloria was just as her mother put it "extremely perceptive," a spy who had somehow infiltrated my graduate classes, or a precocious 13-year-old critic of Rogerian therapy!

At that moment I learned what it really meant to be an effective therapist. I acquiesced with Gloria and explained that reflection and paraphrasing were simply used for the first few minutes and then we would swing into action. In essence I literally changed gears in the midst of the session. I ended up treating Gloria with behavioral techniques such as charting, positive reinforcement, and making her wear three-pound ankle weights on her wrists so she wouldn't unconsciously pull her hair as she watched TV. (She would either stop pulling her hair or would end up with biceps like Arnold Schwarzenegger.) In a very short period of time Gloria was relieved of this *dis-tressing* habit.

On another occasion I was hypnotizing a client. Just as I thought she was becoming extremely relaxed she opened her eyes and said: "I've never told anybody this but I was sexually abused when I was eight years old. Do you think that is something important that we should talk about?" Needless to say, her recollections about her abuse consumed what was left of our session. Insisting we continue with the hypnosis would have been foolish.

In cases like this I tend to believe that the client is generally right in the sense that he or she can tell whether the intervention is productive. In the aforementioned instances I am almost certain that if I had continued with my original game plan, the result would have been less than desirable.

When something isn't working and the client lets you know it, assess the situation at hand and if necessary alter your course of action.

45

Documentation: The Royal Road to Promotion

My friend Martha was furious. For an entire year she threw her heart and soul into being the best child abuse counselor in the office. Her supervisor, however, did not give her a promotion and the raise that went with it.

"What was your supervisor's rationale?" I wanted to know.

"She told me that she doesn't really know what I do when I'm behind closed doors with a client. She goes by what is written in the record and I guess the dictation in my records wasn't all that great."

There's a saying in the helping field suggesting that if you "didn't write it down, it didn't happen." Each year hundreds of workers are penalized for less than desirable documentation skills.

The executive director of a large residential treatment center for children and adolescents once told me that he would hire an individual with a two-year associate's degree over one with a master's degree, if the helper with the two-year degree was a good writer and the one with the master's degree wasn't. A strong statement indeed, but certainly indicative of the importance of the written word in the process of helping others.

Although you needn't write like Faulkner or Hemingway, you must be able to write in a coherent manner that allows others to understand what is transpiring between you and your client.

Here's a neat little trick. If your writing is a little shaky try dictating what you write into a tape recorder. Then listen to it. If it doesn't make sense rewrite it so it does make sense when you listen to the tape. Your supervisor, your client, your self-esteem, and your promotion committee will thank you for it!

46

Avoid Dual Relationships
Like the Plague

Sonya had a 1964 Ford Thunderbird that she drove to work each day. Mr. Townsend, who was in her 10 o'clock assertiveness training group, had his eye on it and told her so. Mr. Townsend was the owner of a restoration garage about 50 miles south of the counseling facility. Before and after group he would explain to Sonya that for just a few hundred dollars he could make some minor repairs and put a few coats of custom metallic paint on her car. He assured her that she would be driving a customized classic that anyone would be proud to own.

The most seductive part of the offer was that Sonya had indeed priced the repairs on her T-Bird, and that, combined with a show-car paint job, would set her back several thousand dollars. The only thing holding her back was the fact that she was Mr. Townsend's therapist. Finally, the urge to restore her dream car was overpowering. "How could it possibly alter the therapy process?" she thought.

Sonya's T-Bird thus ended up in Mr. Townsend's restoration shop; though Sonya thought it looked more like an old barn on his farm when she finally saw it. For two weeks Mr. Townsend mentioned nothing about her car. Sonya was becoming apprehensive and it seemed to be affecting her therapeutic technique. She was responding to Mr. Townsend noticeably less in group and he was speaking up less.

Finally — after four long weeks — Sonya confronted her client about the status of her car. He explained to her that he had been unusually busy and that he really didn't have time to work on her automobile. When Sonya was finally able to get a ride into the country to pick up her vehicle, Mr. Townsend said that he was just charging her $50 for some minor mechanical operations he had performed. When she inquired about specifics, he told her that he did some work on the inside of the left door and made a few adjustments on her automatic transmission. These, needless to say, were repairs that Sonya couldn't verify, and she was convinced the repairs were figments of Mr. Townsend's imagination.

The next day Sonya gave him the evil eye in group, while Mr. Townsend, who had traditionally been verbal, stared at the floor and said nothing. He dropped out of group the next day without explaining his rationale and never came back. Sonya — now a victim of severe countertransference — was secretly happy to see him go.

Sonya was engaging in what is known in the trade as a dual relationship. A dual relationship occurs when a therapist wears two hats. That is to say: Your therapist or helper is also your relative, boyfriend, house painter, or as in the case of Sonya, your customer. In simple terms, the therapist plays the role of your helper, but also plays another role in the client's life.

The best advice I can give any helper — regardless of training or clinical persuasion — regarding dual relationships is to stay away from them. Heed my warning. Nearly every dual relationship will end in disaster. That is why almost all ethical guidelines advise against them.

Recently, however, ethical guidelines have become a tad more liberal when it comes to dual or so-called multiple relationships. These guidelines indicate that the practice may be ethical if you live in a small town where such relationships are unavoidable or constitute the cultural norm. The ethical bodies do emphasize that when you *do* engage in a dual relationship you should make certain that the client is not exploited. If you have a situation that you truly believe falls into these new guidelines, I highly recommend that you discuss the situation with your supervisor, as well as an attorney on your staff or board. Finally, many liability and malpractice carriers now provide practitioners with a toll-free number for ethical and legal advice. This is the ideal situation to take them up on their offer to use this service.

47

Insider Tips for a Good Cover Letter and Human Service Resumé

To sell yourself to an employer or private practice setting, these tips are at least as important as the notes you penned in your theories classes since they could likely help you snare yourself a job. You've no doubt already discovered that those theories aren't overly useful if you don't have a position to practice your craft.

- Always send a cover letter with your resume. Both documents should be typed or word processed on white — or if you're daring, off-white or light gray — cotton bond paper, i.e., paper that has a water mark. Never use a dot matrix printer. Instead rely on a laser or a good ink-jet printer.
- When you write the salutation in your cover letter, rather than using a generic title, such as Dear Director

of Personnel or Dear Clinical Case Management Supervisor, address it to a name such as Mr. John Doe or Dr. Jane Doe. Make certain to spell the individual's name correctly and if the individual has a doctorate, e.g., Ph.D., Ed.D., Psy.D., M.D., D.O. or D.S.W., be certain you use Dear Dr. and not Dear Mr. A lot of folks who have spent years burning the midnight oil to put the letters Dr. before their name get mighty ticked off (more than if you misspelled their name, but of course you'd never do that) when you don't use it. Some could care less, but since you don't know the individual, play it safe and refer to them as doctor. If you are uncertain about spelling or degrees, call the institution in question before sending your cover letter and resume.

- If a person with some connections or clout has recommended you for the job, forget about modesty and say so in the first paragraph. Also be specific about which position you are applying for. Even small agencies often advertise a number of positions concurrently.

- Always send your resume and cover letter in an $8\frac{1}{2}$ by 11 large envelope. Many hospitals and agencies keep the envelopes on all the correspondence received. If you imagine a stack of 100 resumes and cover letters, which really isn't that unusual in today's job market, you can visualize yours — in the largest envelope — that means it is more likely to be read. Moreover, since a resume is a work of art, it must look good, and in addition to being a sale's piece, your materials will remain unfolded.

- If you really want a job badly and aren't exactly certain whether to stress this or that on your resume, you might try a controversial tactic called the split-half method. Send two slightly different resumes, one stressing this and one stressing that. Mail them at different times and under separate cover of course. This technique also lessens the statistical chance that you'll just get passed over since you now have two entries rather than one in the resume stack. If you do secure an interview and the interviewer does catch this anomaly, simply tell him or her the truth that you decided to update your resume.

- Hobbies such as art, word processing, golf, or running a flea-market operation can often help you secure a job at not-for-profit agencies. I remember interviewing two people for the position of volunteer coordinator once. Both were equally qualified, however, one listed flea market sales as her hobby. When I asked her how much money she could raise for our agency by holding a flea-market she assured me that she could bring over a thousand dollars for a day's work. I believed her and after she was hired she more than delivered on her promise. A student of mine who listed desk-top publishing and writing as hobbies was later told that these were the deciding factors that led to her employment because the agency wanted to start a newsletter. Always keep in mind that not-for-profit social service and mental health agencies, unlike large for-profit corporations, often do not have the budget to purchase services that may merely be a pastime for you. Thus an avid golfer could be called upon to coordinate a fund raiser on the links.

- Emphasize the area of your experience relating to the job in question. If, for example, the position is basically an educational one don't focus strictly on clinical experience. You could, for example, list all the courses and/or workshops you have taught. In contrast, a resume listing each and every course you have taught would be inappropriate for a job with a clinical slant.

- If your professional experience in the field is minimal, create a heading such as Relevant Experience and list your practicum, internship, clerkship, or volunteer experience. Notice the heading is truthful in that it neither says nor implies that you were an employee or paid for the experience. Remember that your time flipping burgers or waiting on tables often isn't enough. I have numerous students who send out resumes that depict no experience because they have never had a job in the field. Many of these students have had a myriad of service learning experiences and fail to list them on the resume because they were unpaid positions.
- If your resume and cover letter do the job, and you land an interview and really want the job, immediately send a thank you letter to the interviewer.

48

If You Are Daydreaming, Your Client Will Perceive You as an Uninterested Helper

It's 15 minutes into the interview and your client has been droning on and on about her countless squabbles with her younger sister. This is a familiar tale of woe that you've heard more times than you care to remember. At times you could finish the sentences for her.

As a fallible human, your mind begins to wander. When your own personal daydream ends your client is still babbling on about her relationship difficulties. For a moment you wonder if your client noticed that your mind was a million miles away.

"No," you conclude, "I'm certain she didn't know the difference." Don't be so sure.

There's a neat little exercise I perform with my college theories and skills class every semester. Everyone in the room picks a partner. One person plays the helper, the other the client. Then I separate the two groups. I explain to the client-group that unbeknownst to the helper-group they will be rating their therapists on a scale of one to 100. An average helper, I explain, should be rated as a 50. A helper who is absolutely perfect should receive a rating of 100, while a therapist who is your worst nightmare can be given a rating of one.

Next I speak to the helper-group in private and explain they will have two brief four-minute mini-sessions with their client. Unbeknownst to the client-group I admonish the help-ers to *purposely* allow their minds to wander during the initial trial. With the second trial, however, the helpers are told to hang onto every word the client says, no matter how difficult that might be.

Certainly you can guess what happens every time. When the helper is not listening the client notices it, perhaps even unconsciously, and rates the person playing the counselor significantly lower than in the second trial. In fact, it isn't that unusual to have a person receive a score of zero and then a score hovering around the 100 mark.

This principle is pervasive in the sense that it transcends any theory of counseling, therapy, or intervention you use.

It is thus imperative to remember that whether you want to admit it or not, your client will notice if you're not paying attention. So tune in and turn your client on to efficacious treatment.

Pick a Theory of Intervention and a Job You Believe In

When I finished my master's degree I saw an advertisement for a hypnotist at a new smoking cessation center. When I arrived at the interview, the owner of the practice excused himself and said he would return momentarily which he did. Much to my surprise he now had a cigarette in his mouth and was puffing away. The rest of the pack was peeking out of the pocket from his white dress shirt.

The shock must have shown on my face for he smiled slyly and boasted, "Hey, Rosenthal. Don't look so darn shocked. This is a luxury I don't have during the day. I don't really believe in my product, do you?"

Here was someone hawking "stop smoking via hypnosis" who not only smoked but didn't *even* believe in hypnosis. It was kind of like finding out that the new car salesman who sold you a new Chevrolet really drives a Ford. He went on to explain at length how much money he expected to make with his hypnosis scheme.

I didn't take the job and privately prognosticated that his center would be out of business in six months. Actually, I overestimated his longevity. He closed up shop in six weeks. Now I don't know it for a fact but I can almost bet you that the clients (consciously or unconsciously) could sense that this snake-oil peddler didn't believe in his product. And if you don't believe in your product, I'm betting you can't sell it to your client. What's more, I don't care if the product is hypnosis, family therapy, NLP, TA, REBT, behavior therapy, or anything else you could conjure up.

In another example of my helping philosophy and vocational choice, a young lady from a residential treatment center came to one of my undergraduate classes in an attempt to recruit volunteers and practicum students. At the time, her site had a reputation as the most popular volunteer/practicum agency in the city. Thus, selling my students on the idea of using her facility should have been a piece of cake. As the representative gave her sales pitch I could sense that deep down she didn't believe in what they were doing. Something was obviously wrong. In fact, I couldn't help but think that I could have easily done a better job of firing the students up and I wasn't even working for her agency.

Not surprisingly, although she spoke with my three largest classes not a single student chose to work at her center. Some of the students remarked that she seemed ambivalent about the center although to be sure everything she said about the facility was positive. Somehow, her nonverbal communication was telegraphing a different message to the students and me. At the time I remember wondering if there was a way I could confirm my suspicions without asking her.

About two weeks later I was shopping in a discount store and ran into her. She immediately began by telling me that she was no longer an employee of the center. She quit because she really didn't like the way they were handling the clients and it was causing her discord. Although she confided that she had not as yet found another job and her bank account was falling rapidly she was convinced she made the right move getting out. She seemed surprised when I told her that her real feelings were evident during her presentation.

If you don't believe in yourself, your treatment modality, or your agency, neither will your clients.

50

Despite the Pitfalls, Make Friends with the Media to Promote Yourself and Your Agency

My friends and family were gathered in my living room hovering around the television with a large bag of popcorn, a bowl of chips, and plenty of soft drinks. Everyone gazed at the clock as it moved toward the magic five o'clock hour. Earlier that day a massive news truck from a major TV station, replete with a satellite dish on top, had been parked in our driveway. I had given the anchorwoman a report that would be aired in a few moments.

"Look you're on the air," shouted my wife Patti. Much to everyone's chagrin, there I was on the 32-inch screen espousing my thoughts on mental health when everyone in the room, including me, broke into a fit of hysterical laughter. The caption identified me as my colleague in practice next door. When I called the station to protest, the fellow who took my call chuckled and said that it would not be rectified for the 10 o'clock edition. Just for the record, he was correct.

The media can be your friend or your foe; they can make or break your reputation. I've always tried to cooperate with the press. When I worked as the program director for a local crisis center, television, radio, and newspaper articles helped immensely in terms of keeping us supplied with volunteers and donors. On other occasions the media has helped me secure private practice clients, sell books, and garner lecture engagements. All in all, the media can do a great deal to promote your practice and/or agency.

Nevertheless, I urge you not to get your hopes up too high for I can almost guarantee you will be sadly disappointed if you don't expect a number of minor or perhaps even major glitches to occur when you deal with the media. Let me share a few of the most common ones.

- I have been interviewed for newspaper articles that appeared in the smallest freebie county periodicals to the largest newspapers in the U.S., for example, the *National Enquirer* and *USA Today*. In most of the articles something I said was taken out of context or I was misquoted. You should expect the same. I still find it humorous that one newspaper quoted me as saying that "10 out of every hundred kids will commit suicide." If that were true we wouldn't have many kids left. On one occasion after giving a lecture in a small town, the front page lead story had a huge picture of me pointing my finger at the reader. The caption beneath the photo read, to my horror, "Counselor blames society for teen suicide."
- When conducting long drawn-out interviews with television and/or cable news reporters, you should realize that the actual time you will appear on TV will be incredibly short — if your interview appears

at all. Incidentally, when your interview is butchered or doesn't air, don't take your anger out on the reporter who interviewed you. The final results, and this is true for print media as well, have often been decided by editors, producers, and program managers. Also a big local or national story will often preempt or postpone your piece and keep it out of the media. If the largest building in town catches fire or a national figure dies, don't expect to see yourself on the tube that night talking about reality therapy groups.

- Have you ever seen a nationally known expert appear on a television talk show and thought, I could have done a better job answering that question? Don't be so sure. Unbeknownst to you, as well as the rest of the viewing audience, is that at the very moment the expert began to answer the question a card was flashed in front of him or her stating, "30 seconds until the commercial." Mentally prepare for this situation since there's a good chance you will come face to face with it, if and when you grace the silver screen.

- Do not make the assumption that national shows are better to deal with than those on a local level. I could relate a number of dreadful horror stories, but I will limit my discussion to a few well-chosen examples. After I spent six weeks helping a national talk show prepare a show, I was told when I arrived at the studio that there was only room for the clients on the set, but I was welcome to sit back stage and watch the program on the monitor. I had been told upfront that I would be the expert on the show that day. Hey, thanks guys. That's really kind. In a number of instances shows have called me literally begging me to help them secure a client for a given segment related to mental health or counseling. I was told that if I could secure a client for a given show they would plug one of my books. "Imagine the exposure your book will get," they reminded me. "It would cost you thousands in advertising." The media is correct about one thing. I have always resorted to imagination. I have *never* had a show on the national level follow through on this promise even on occasions when they said I needed to overnight express books to the program manager, at my cost of nearly $100. Local shows, however, have occasionally followed through in this regard.

- Think twice before you recommend a client for a talk show. A client I recommended for a national talk show was told during a commercial break that the audience and the advertisers wanted her to scream and cry. My client protested that she thought this show was devoted to those who had problems and were now able to take charge of their emotions. An 18-year-old client of mine did an interview for another national show the same day the Gulf War broke out. Since her segment was not used the day it was filmed she was told to call the show daily long distance — at her expense — to discover whether the show was going to air on that particular day. After six months her mother decided they could no longer afford the daily long-distance call. About a year later a friend of hers called to say that she had seen her on national television and luckily had been video taping the show that day. This national show never even had the courtesy to call my client to inform her when she was going to be on the air.

The media can help you reach thousands, if not millions, of individuals who you could never reach otherwise. Just remember that when you deal with the media, Murphy's Law, which asserts that if something can go wrong it will, seems to be in full force. Also — and this is crucial — it is imperative that you ask your supervisor what the agency or hospital communication policy is regarding the media. Many agencies have strict policies regarding who can and cannot speak with the media. In addition, your supervisor or director may issue a statement for all staff if an incident attracts media attention. Find out before you do the wrong thing and get yourself in hot water.

51

Writing a Book or Starting a Project? Ask Your Agency First

Rebecca Simms had spent the last four years of her life creating an innovative therapeutic game to help co-dependent women. Needless to say, she was absolutely delighted when a large company bought the game from her for a significant amount of money.

To celebrate, Rebecca decided to take her executive director of the counseling agency where she worked at out to lunch. When Rebecca broke the news to her director she was taken aback by her director's reaction. Instead of praising or congratulating Rebecca, her director was downright mean and hostile. Her director castigated her for not telling her about the project sooner and told Rebecca that any money or royalties she received would go to the agency. Was Rebecca's experience atypical? Hardly. Many agencies have an even more inflexible and stern policy.

Some agencies have a strict policy that anything you create, such as a book, a pamphlet, an assessment device, a cassette tape, or video, that is related to mental health or social service becomes the property of the agency. In fact, your agency may even copyright the product under the agency's name. One rationale is that the agency is paying you to create the product or document. However, I must point out that some agencies assume ownership of your product even if you created your product totally on your own time.

If you have a project in mind and don't want your agency to steal your idea, glory, royalties, or hard work, then I recommend you discuss your project *before* you sign on the dotted line to take the job. In fact, I would probably take the matter one step further and have your agency, hospital, school, or practice sign a legal agreement created by your attorney that clearly states your rights and ownership in regard to your creation. What do you do if your current or future place of employment won't sign the contract? Well, that's up to you and how committed you are to your project. For example, I know of one case where a professional quit his job so he could write a book and keep the royalties.

The same basic principle applies when you are starting your own practice. Here again, your employer could specify that you cannot practice in the same vicinity or catchment area. Others may flat out stipulate that you cannot have an outside practice at all if you are employed at their facility. Unfortunately most helpers never bother to research such matters prior to securing employment. The good news is that you won't be one of them.

52

Your Employment and Credentials Determine What You Pay for Malpractice Insurance

Following college, I secured employment at a state agency where we would routinely transport clients in our automobiles. For over 10 years my colleagues and I repeatedly asked if we were covered in the event of an accident happening with a client or clients. Despite our pleas for an answer we were always told that they (whoever "they" were) would get back to us. The reason we wanted coverage from our employer was that our personal auto insurance premiums would have gone sky high if we asked for coverage to transport clients.

Finally, I called my insurance agent who chuckled and said, "Howard, if you were covered, they would simply tell you that you were covered."

It is also a gross misconception to assume that your agency has a malpractice policy, or what is often called professional liability, which covers you. I remember when I was the program director for a helpline and our insurance company informed us that (at least at that time) we were one of only a handful of centers in the U.S. that had malpractice for staff and volunteers.

A lot of factors affect the price you will pay for malpractice insurance. Students usually pay considerably less than licensed professionals. When comparing licensed professionals, social workers usually pay the lowest fees. Licensed counselors generally pay a higher rate and those persons who are licensed as psychologists pay the stiffest price tags. The type of work you do also makes a huge difference.

Let's take an actual example. As I write this page I am looking at an insurance rate card for professional counselors. A full-time counselor employed in a K–12 school would pay $263 a year for a $2-million claim/$4-million aggregate claim policy. If that same counselor drops to 15 hours or less a week, then he or she is considered part-time and the rate drops to $197. If that same counselor is employed at an agency, practice, or hospital the rate shoots up to $431 or $323 for a part-timer. If that same counselor decides to take the big step and go into private practice, or what the insurance company calls a "self-employed counselor," then the counselor will now pay a whopping $573 or $430 for 15 hours a week or less.

Now if you were peering over my shoulder at this moment you might look at the rate card and comment that our self-employed counselor could save a bundle — $253 full-time or $190 part-time — by taking a $200,000/$200,000 policy. You could assert that in your concerted opinion the counselor doesn't realistically need that mega $2-million/$4-million policy. Unfortunately, even if you are correct it probably won't matter. You see managed care companies often stipulate how much insurance self-employed practitioners must carry and I have to admit I haven't seen any recently with the $200,000/$200,000 cost-effective bargain-basement rate policy. The minimum is usually $1-million/$3-million or the aforementioned $2-million/$4-million policy.

Therapists who supervise others, do hypnosis, or work with psychotic clients may also be asked to pay a higher rate. Interestingly enough, the direction that a profession chooses to take could also have a profound influence on what you pay. For example, psychologists have been trying to secure the right to dispense psychiatric medicinals for a number of years. Now that some areas are allowing psychologists to prescribe medicine, I can guarantee you that these psychologists will see drastic increases in their malpractice insurance premiums.

There is no way to beat the system, nevertheless, there are a few ways to make it more palatable. Professional organizations, such as the American Counseling Association (ACA), nearly always offer policies to members. I have found that as a general rule these organizations provide helpers a fair deal. Their rates are generally lower than competitors simply because they are buying a huge number of policies. However, they will usually stipulate that you must be a member of their organization to be eligible for a policy. When you figure the price of the membership plus the policy price, the total bill is often almost identical to the price you would pay if you went directly through a malpractice carrier. Thus, even though you really end up paying almost the same price, you're getting a membership (usually replete with newsletters, journals, discounts on conferences, and other perks) thrown in. Organizations sometimes offer discounts for certifications or attending workshops they sponsor pertaining to legal or ethical matters.

Malpractice insurance companies who specialize in this field and advertise in professional publications, and professional organizations, such as ACA, will invariably offer you a better deal than what your friendly neighborhood insurance company can secure for you.

My advice in terms of securing malpractice insurance is the antithesis of my advice regarding the use of strong therapeutic confrontation: sooner is definitely better than later. Get coverage now. You won't regret it.

53

Private Practice Is Not a Panacea for Everything That Ails You

I remember as if it happened yesterday. It was the early 1970s and I was sitting in my abnormal psychology class. I leaned over and asked a student who worked as a teacher's aide at the university why our abnormal psychology professor missed class every time we had an exam. I figured that since the aide rubbed elbows with the faculty he might just have the inside scoop.

My cohort furrowed his brow and whispered, "You really don't know?" When I forthrightly admitted my ignorance, he replied, "The guy's in private practice and he charges 50 smackers an hour, man."

I was dumbfounded. I didn't know anybody who made $50 an hour. I decided right then that I wanted to devote my life to helping others and I might as well do it with an overinflated bank account. For several years I almost forgot about my goal of being in private practice but remembered it instantly after I landed my first job as a caseworker. My monthly salary was in the $500 range and that was before Uncle Sam took his share. When I began to worry that my bank was going to charge me a search fee for my deposits, private practice emerged in my conscious mind once again.

Today — over 20 years later — the situation has not changed appreciably. Most new students, and helpers in agencies, hospitals, and schools still see private practice as a panacea, somewhat of a goldmine: Set your own hours, see the clients you want to see, and do your own thing while watching the cash roll in. Nice fantasy, but hardly based in reality. While it is true that the average salary for private practitioners is often higher than those who are employed, the numbers are highly misleading.

Who makes more: the therapist who is self-employed and rakes in $50,000 a year or the employed therapist who makes $35,000? The private practitioner will have to buy his own health insurance. Then he or she will need office space, furniture, a secretary, a phone system, a telephone answering system or service, a phone book ad, business cards, stationery, malpractice insurance, workshop fees, and a slew of other things that are paid for by nearly any employer. Let's assume that the therapist is working under a *percentage split* (see Tip #1, Join Forces with a Psychiatrist to Open a Risk-Free Private Practice) with a psychiatrist or other mental health specialist and all of the aforementioned factors are paid for. (Although the likelihood of medical insurance being paid for would be exceedingly low.) Even if the split was 70 percent for the therapist and 30 percent for the office services, the therapist would have to make $50,000 from clients' fees to take in $35,000. That means that you would need to conduct approximately 666 sessions a year or 13 sessions a week at $70 per client.

Now at first glance the act of conducting 13 sessions per week to make $35,000 a year seems rather easy. In fact, you might appropriately point out that most practitioners charge more than $70 a session and thus you could work even less. That's where you'd be wrong. First, how many managed care companies pay $70 or $80 per hour for individual therapy? Ask a few of your friends in private practice, I think you'll be surprised and I don't mean pleasantly surprised. I have dealt with some that pay less than $40 per hour — yes, even if you have the title of doctor before your name.

What's more, $35,000 a year assumes every single client pays every penny of his or her bill. In this regard I can tell you that some clients do and others don't. When I left my last office my clients owed me over $13,000 that I will never see.

How do I know I'll never see it? These are people that were kindly told they needed to pay the bill. Then they were told we could work out a payment plan with them. Then they were given a limited time to make a payment before they were turned over to collections. The next step was to hire a collection agency. When the collection agency did everything they legally could the tab was a little over $13,000.

Dreamer that I am, I still believed these clients would make some payments. I thus sent a kind letter to everyone and told them they were no longer in collection. I further pointed out that I would only write them once and they could pay me whatever they could afford or thought was fair. I emphasized that they could send anything — even five dollars — and I would close their account in good standing. I further provided a return envelope. Can you imagine what you would do if you owed a credit card company say a couple thousand dollars and they sent you a letter like that? I know what I'd do. I'd call and ask if the company had made a mistake.

Colleagues and fellow college instructors thought it was an interesting experiment and nearly everyone I spoke with predicted that almost every client would send me something. At the end of the process one client — that's it one — sent me $30 on a rather large bill and his check bounced. He did, however, remit a money order after I informed him what transpired. Nobody else even bothered to call or write me.

Only one of my peers could empathize. A fellow who was in private practice next door to me revealed that he quit practicing in the area when clients owed him in excess of $20,000. "I couldn't stand the countertransference," he sheepishly remarked.

Incidentally, I take full responsibility for this fiasco. I enabled clients to run up astronomical bills — one in excess of $2,400 — by not enforcing payment. Since that time I've become strict about collecting outstanding balances and I advise you to do the same. You'll lose more clients, but you won't be seeing all your clients *pro bono*. A wise policy is simply to tell the clients that you can't see them unless their bill is current. A lot of nonprofit agencies live by this credo too.

The self-employed practitioner needs to ask her or himself some important questions. What happens when she takes a cruise for a two-week summer vacation? How much income has she brought in during that period? Nothing that isn't residual. An employed practitioner generally gets vacation pay. What if she misses a day, or worse yet, several weeks or months due to illness or pregnancy? Here too, full-time agency workers generally accrue sick-leave benefits. What happens when there's snow on the ground and it's too slick to go out for a few days? The full-time employed counselor, on the other hand, gets the usual check even if the agency shuts down for inclement weather. What happens when a helper working in private practice has six clients scheduled and it's a beautiful summer-like day in the middle

146

of the winter and everybody decides to play hooky and go on a picnic? Again, no money comes in. When you work full-time at an agency, at a hospital, or as a school counselor you still get a check even when no clients wander through the door.

And remember, even if the private therapist never takes a day off and collects every dime he or she has coming, the individual still won't receive any benefits. Thus, if a private practitioner wants to make the same as an agency, school, or hospital helper he or she needs to make a heck of a lot more in net income.

Since it may well sound like I am bad-mouthing private practice let me clarify my position. I am not. In fact, for many years that is precisely what I did for the bulk of my income. The flexibility and prestige are nice. Overall, however, I don't think it is any better or worse than employed positions. Both have their pluses as well as their drawbacks. Yes, there are a lot of private practitioners who command high six-figure incomes, nevertheless, many self-employed helpers are in the same class as starving artists. The ones who are really raking in the big bucks are usually those who have a number of therapists working for them, either for salary or a percentage split, or they have magnificent referral sources.

54

Steer Clear of False Memory Syndrome

Client: "My symptoms are really strange. What do you think is going on here?"

Therapist: "Well quite frankly your situation really isn't all that unusual."

Client: "You're serious?"

Therapist: "Absolutely. It occurs in a high percentage of women."

Client: "Well what is it?"

Therapist: "I'm afraid you were sexually abused as a child."

Client: "Oh, my god! Are you sure?"

Therapist: "Like I say, I've seen this pattern in women before."

Client: "Yes, but I mean … um … I don't remember ever being sexually abused."

Therapist: "And that would go along with the theory."

Client: "Theory? What theory?"

Therapist: "The one that asserts that sexual abuse is such a horrendous trauma that the victim — in this case you — represses the entire memory."

Client: "Oh my god. So it was so painful I forgot it."

Therapist: "Yes. Not on purpose or anything. I mean your mind is just trying to protect you."

Client: "I know you truly know your field, but are you sure?"

Therapist: "It certainly makes sense doesn't it?"

Client: "I guess … yes, I guess it does."

This is a blatant example of a therapist leading the client and bad treatment. Here the therapist finds exactly what he or she expects to find. Unfortunately, the client has not provided the raw material to make such a finding. This helper has induced a condition known as False Memory Syndrome (FMS), the subject of numerous professional and popular articles in the media. In at least one case FMS made the cover of a national magazine that rarely if ever dabbles in psychotherapeutic topics.

The rule regarding FMS is succinct and to the point: steer clear of it. Do not — I repeat — do not put words or ideas in the client's head. First, the practice is unethical and, secondly, because you could easily create a problem for the helpee that never existed in the first place. If a client comes to his or her own conclusion that a memory has been repressed that's fine — not to mention highly therapeutic. Nevertheless, your job is to avoid planting any seeds.

55

Create an Emotional Trophy Closet to Help You Through a Bad Day

If you believe in creative visualization, imagine this day. The client you felt you were helping the most yells at you and tells you you're in the wrong profession. A second client, whom you thought was making progress, calls you three times because she is contemplating suicide. Your supervisor calls you in and questions your judgment regarding a recent therapeutic decision, and last but not least the mailman hand delivers a certified letter to you with a return receipt postcard indicating that a client — yes, the one you felt you did the most for — is suing you for malpractice.

You can bet you won't feel elated when you get home. Especially not after the local traffic cop gave you a ticket for making a rolling stop after you left your client's house where you were kind enough to conduct a home-visit therapy session.

What usually happens after one of these trying days is that the individual feels badly. Doubt sets in and the helper begins to wonder if he or she is inept. Perhaps she even reaches emotional rock bottom, questioning if this is the right field for her.

At this point I highly recommend my *emotional trophy closet strategy*.

An emotional trophy closet is merely a collection of your successes. You could easily compile an emotional trophy closet in a shoe box, a file drawer cabinet, or a three-ring binder. The emotional trophy closet consists of items intended to build your professional self-esteem and self-confidence.

You may want to include in your emotional trophy closet some of the following items. You might have a note or a rating from your supervisor (yes, the same one that questioned your therapeutic judgment earlier in the day) that lauded your commendable performance. Perhaps you have a thank-you card from a client, patient, student, or fellow worker. Certificates of achievement are also highly recommended. An article from the local county journal could also be a part of it. Include anything and everything that makes you feel positive. If an item directly states or implies that you are a competent, accomplished professional then use it! This is no time for modesty!

The next time your spirits dip or you question your abilities make a bee line for the closet. Remember to keep adding new and exciting treasures. After spending 10 minutes in your closet you'll feel like a new man or woman.

Conclusion

I gathered my materials from the podium and walked out the door of my Introduction to Human Services class. The hall was empty except for two of my students who were passively awaiting my exit.

The young woman was 19 with light brown hair pulled back into a pony tail. The young man was 22, clean cut and closely cropped hair. He wanted to work in law enforcement and to be sure he already looked the part. Earlier in the semester, she had shared her aspiration to work with troubled kids, primarily those who had sustained sexual abuse.

The young woman looked into my eyes with a degree of sincerity one does not often encounter. She asked, "Why do you do it, Dr. Rosenthal?"

"Yeah," said the young man, "I mean why do you still do it? You don't have to."

The couple was referring to the fact that in addition to my full-time college teaching schedule I still counsel a handful of clients each Saturday in my private practice.

As I looked into their inquisitive eyes, I knew that I was looking at myself more than 20 years ago.

The real question was why should anybody, including us, go into this profession. These students were seeking a serious answer. They needed an answer that came deep from the heart. Quoting a job description from the *Dictionary of Occupational Titles* or some government figures regarding potential openings in the coming years was not what they needed to hear.

I told them the following story: In 1974, I was doing casework for the state. I was young, about your age. One of my clients was a middle-aged woman who was living on public assistance and food stamps in an impoverished section of the city. Each time I visited her home she would read from her personal diary and on each occasion I was struck by the fact that this woman was an extremely talented writer. I repeatedly emphasized that she had a gift and I urged her to cultivate it by taking a writing course at the community college located just minutes from her house. Unfortunately, my recommendation was always met with resistance.

"Aw, I'm just another old welfare client, Mr. Rosenthal," she would protest. "Nobody in my family has ever set a foot in a college and I suspect I won't be any different."

Each time I thought I was about to make a breakthrough her low self-esteem would show its ugly teeth. Like a man on a proverbial treadmill my client was stuck. She was literally a prisoner of her mind, held captive by her own self-limiting belief system that dictated who she was and worse yet what she could accomplish.

Then what seemed like an extended period of time went by before I heard from her. One day she called and insisted that I visit her at once. When I arrived, she smiled with an ear-to-ear grin as she carefully handed me a newspaper.

"What do you think?" she asked. As I glanced at the periodical, I could see that I was holding the local community college newspaper. My eyes began to scan the page but came to a screeching halt as they landed on a story by —

you guessed it — my client. What came next was even more remarkable. Her story entitled *No More Night Snooping* was an article about … me! The piece talked about how I was representative of a new breed of caseworker who really tries to help the client rather than the typical caseworker of the past who visited the home at night to see if welfare mothers were hiding a man in the house.

As I looked up, I detected tears in the eyes of my two neophyte students. I knew they understood. And that, my dear reader, is why I still help people. That's why I keep coming back for more. Some people, even if they are a minority, do appreciate it. There are those whose lives we change forever — they know it and they cherish it.

This is a challenging field with rich emotional rewards. Hopefully these 55 key ideas, conspicuously missing from my own education, will help you avoid the land mines and guide you on your fascinating journey as a helper. Hey, let's get together some time and swap emotional trophy closet stories.